C. P. CAVAFY

The Unfinished Poems

C. P. ÇAVAFY

The Unfinished Poems

THE FIRST ENGLISH TRANSLATION,

WITH INTRODUCTION AND COMMENTARY,

BY

DANIEL MENDELSOHN

BASED ON THE GREEK EDITION OF RENATA LAVAGNINI

ALFRED A. KNOPF
NEW YORK

—

2009

THIS IS A BORZOI BOOK
PUBLISHED BY ALFRED A. KNOPF

Introduction, notes, commentary, and translation copyright © 2009
by Daniel Mendelsohn

Frontispiece art courtesy The Cavafy Archive/Manuel Savidis

The poems and fragmentary sketches in this work were first published in a Greek edi-
tion, *Ateli,* by Ikaros Publishers, Athens, in 1994 with arrangement and commentary
by Renata Lavagnini, translations of which are published here with new commentary by
Daniel Mendelsohn. The Greek-language poems are copyright © by Manuel Savidis.

Grateful acknowledgment is made to Harvard University Press and the Trustees of the
Loeb Classical Library for permission to reprint an excerpt from *Philostratus: Volume I,*
Loeb Classical Library® Volume 16, translated by Christopher P. Jones (Cambridge,
Mass.: Harvard University Press), copyright © 2005 by The President and Fellows of
Harvard College. The Loeb Classical Library® is a registered trademark of the President
and Fellows of Harvard College. Reprinted by permission of Harvard University Press
and the Trustees of the Loeb Classical Library.

The poem "It Must Have Been the Spirits" originally appeared in *The New Yorker.*

Library of Congress Cataloging-in-Publication Data
Cavafy, Constantine, 1863–1933.
[Poems. English. Selections]
The unfinished poems / C. P. Cavafy ; the first English translation, with introduction
and commentary, by Daniel Mendelsohn.
p. cm.
Translation of: Atele poiemata, 1918–1932 / K. P. Kavaphes ; philologike ekdose kai
scholia, Renata Lavagnini.
"This is a Borzoi book."
Includes bibliographical references.
ISBN 978-0-307-26546-3
1. Cavafy, Constantine, 1863–1933—Translations into English.
I. Mendelsohn, Daniel Adam, 1960–
II. Lavagnini, Renata.   III.   Title.
PA5610.K2A2 2009b
889'.132—dc22   2008034717

Manufactured in the United States of America
First Edition

CONTENTS

CONTENTS

INTRODUCTION

IN THE AUTUMN OF 1932, at the end of a four-month sojourn in Athens that also marked the beginning of the end of his life, Constantine Cavafy revealed with some agitation that he had important unfinished business to attend to. "I still have twenty-five poems to write," he declared to some friends, in the distorted whisper to which his famously mellifluous and enchanting voice had been reduced following the tracheotomy that was meant to save him from throat cancer, and which was the reason he'd come to Athens from Alexandria. "Twenty-five poems!"

The conversation, recalled by one of the friends to whom he'd spoken that day and reported after Cavafy's death in April of the following year, was merely the first of what turned out to be several tantalizing references to a body of unfinished work that the poet was desperately trying to complete as death closed in. Ten years later, in 1943, someone who'd been engaged in compiling Cavafy's bibliography during the very year in which the poet had traveled to Athens seeking medical help revealed that Cavafy had made it plain to him that the bibliography was far from complete. In 1963, on the thirtieth anniversary of Cavafy's death, someone else wrote in to a newspaper claiming that, during those last months, the dying poet had written him to say that he still had fifteen poems to finish.

The mysterious texts to which these various hints alluded were finally identified, also in 1963, by the scholar George Savidis, Cavafy's great editor, after an inspection of the Cavafy Archive, which Savidis himself eventually came to possess after acquiring it from Cavafy's friend and heir, Alexander Sengopoulos. A year later, in an article about material in the Archive that had yet to be published (some of which—a number of poems that Cavafy had completed but did not approve for publication—he would publish in 1968 as "The Unpublished Poems"),

Savidis revealed, with the deep emotion of an archaeologist making a great discovery, the existence of a cache of incomplete drafts, composed between 1918 and 1932, that the poet had left, meticulously labeled and organized, among his papers:

> More interesting still are the sketches of 25 poems that Cavafy was unable to finish, and on which he was working, with great difficulty, during the last months of his life. Carefully wrapped by him in makeshift envelopes, each with its provisional title and the date, I imagine, of its first conception, they proceed from 1918 to 1932, and along with the very full drafts of some of the published work (like "Caesarion") and some of the unpublished but completed poems, they give us a unique, unhoped-for, and tremendously moving look at the stages of Cavafian creation.

Closer inspection eventually revealed that there were, in fact, thirty drafts in all, along with a handful of fragmentary texts. In time, Savidis entrusted the task of editing these drafts, some of them awaiting the most minor of finishing touches, others apparently in the final stages of preparation but complicated by various textual problems, to the Italian scholar Renata Lavagnini. A professor of Modern Greek at the University of Palermo and member of the Istituto Siciliano di Studi Bizantini e Neoellenici (the Sicilian Institute of Byzantine and Modern Greek Studies, founded by her father, the great Byzantinist and Neohellenist Bruno Lavagnini), she is both an authority on the literary aspects of Cavafy's work and a meticulous philologist. As a specialist in textual criticism, Professor Lavagnini was particularly well equipped to tackle the technical problems associated with editing a mass of manuscript drafts into coherent texts—although, as she herself would be the first to emphasize, these texts must always remain, at best, hypothetical; something the reader must bear in mind.

The heroic task of sifting through these sometimes illegible sketches, of teasing out, from crossed-out lines and scribbled-in insertions, each discrete stage (or, as the poet called it, *morfí,* "form") in the evolution of a given poem, of arriving at the likely last form taken by each work, and of meticulously annotating textual issues, as well as providing a thoroughgoing literary and historical commentary, took decades, but there can be no doubt that the result was worth the wait. The fruits of Professor Lavagnini's labor, published as a scholarly Greek edition in 1994, gives this important body of poetic work to the world in a definitive form; it bears the title chosen by Savidis, by which it will hereafter be known: *Ateli piimata,* the "Unfinished Poems." (The adjective *ateli* in Greek suggests, too, a state of "imperfection.") Thanks to the generous cooperation of the Cavafy Archive, the present volume now makes this vitally important addition to our understanding of one of the twentieth century's greatest poets available to English speakers for the first time.

The Unfinished Poems are unusual in at least one crucial respect. More often than not, when previously unknown manuscripts by major authors unexpectedly come to light, the material in question is juvenilia: immature work from the earliest phase of the artist's career, which he or she has discarded or repressed and which, either through the dogged detective work of dedicated scholars or through happy accidents, suddenly sees the light of day once more. The discovery, in 1994, of Louisa May Alcott's first novel, which languished in the Harvard University Library until it was discovered by a pair of professors researching Alcott's papers, and the 2004 discovery of the complete draft of an early novel of Truman Capote among some papers and photographs that had passed into the hands of a former house sitter, are but two recent examples. And yet as exciting and dramatic as these revelations can be, such work tends, inevitably, to be interesting less for any inherent artistic value it possesses than for the light it can shed on the writer's creative development.

The thirty Unfinished Poems of Cavafy, by contrast, represent the last and greatest phase of the poet's career: the decade and a half from 1918, when Cavafy was fifty-five—and when, too, he published the first of his "sensual" (or "aesthetic") poems that were explicitly homosexual in nature—until the year before his death at the age of seventy. For this reason they are of the deepest significance not merely inasmuch as they illuminate the existing works that constitute the *Collected Poems*—the one hundred and fifty-four Published Poems; the seventy-seven Unpublished Poems; and the Repudiated Poems, twenty-seven verses (and several translations) published early in his career and then renounced on aesthetic grounds after the rigorous 1903–04 "Philosophical Scrutiny" of his work—but as serious works of art in themselves, the deeply wrought products of a great poetic consciousness at its peak.

The publication of a writer's unfinished work is, inevitably, an enterprise that raises complicated questions. This is particularly true in the case of a writer like Cavafy, who ruthlessly culled his own work every year, suppressing everything that did not meet his exacting standards— and who, as I describe in detail in my Introduction to the *Collected Poems,* often waited years before publishing a poem, continually revising and refining it (and continuing to do so, in fact, even after publication), all of which suggests a stringent adherence to the very highest criteria of polish and perfection. But there is persuasive evidence that Cavafy considered the thirty drafts presented here as work he eventually meant to be recognized and published. The Cavafy Archive contains two lists that the poet made of work in progress: one dates to 1930, and the other was kept and constantly revised between 1923 and 1932. The former contains the titles of twenty-nine poems, of which twenty-five are all of the Unfinished drafts he'd composed by that time, and the latter records the titles of fifty poems, a figure that includes all thirty of the Unfinished drafts. All of the other poems listed in these indices are works Cavafy eventually sent to the printer. Hence the lists strongly indicate that the poet—who, as we know from the manuscripts of his Unpublished Poems, was perfectly willing to mark a finished poem with a note declaring that it "need not be published. But it may continue remaining here. It does not deserve to be suppressed"—made no distinction between those poems that he published and the ones he did not, in the end, have time to complete and publish. It was only time, and finally death, that consigned them, for a while, to obscurity.

"Light on one poem, partial light on another." Cavafy's 1927 remark is nowhere more apt than in the case of the Unfinished Poems. In my Introduction to the *Collected Poems,* I explore at some length the remarkable process by which Cavafy, between the ages of thirty and forty, transformed himself from a mediocre poet—one who used the ancient past, evoked in highly perfumed and indeed fashionably "Byzantine" verse, as a kind of exotic scrim to conceal rather than explore his burning preoccupations (intellectual as well as erotic; Hellenic history and identity as well as Greek love)—into a great one, one who came to understand that his large and urgent subject *was* the past: not simply the intriguing or exotic or poignant histories of empires or of lovers, but in particular the way that only the passage of time lays bare, often too late, the truths that politics or passions in the present often conceal from us. There, I contemplate the way in which Cavafy's famous penchant for the margins—of history (Byzantium and Late Antiquity rather than the Age of Pericles or the Rome of the Caesars) and of geography (Antioch rather than Athens; Cyrene, Commagene, and Cappadocia rather than the Capitoline Hill)—well served Cavafy's distinctive poetical-historical vision, allowing him to enjoy a special, outsider's perspective on the decay of civilizations and desires; one with which, as a diaspora, Alexandrian Greek—and, naturally, as a homosexual—he was already all too familiar.

That special perspective is what allowed Cavafy to achieve his unique tone, at once sardonic and compassionate, world-weary and often disappointed, but also so movingly forgiving of the weaknesses and vanities and foibles in his characters—kings, generals, pretentious poetasters, lovers, rent-boys—to which he knew we are all subject. The perspective and the tone, in fact, blur the lines between the "historical" and the "erotic" poetry—an invidious distinction, as I argue, that obscures our sense of his large project. For this self-described "poet-historian" did not, as it so often appears, have two subjects—present desire and the ancient past—but looked at the decline of civilizations dead for a thousand years and the end of love affairs that sputtered only months ago with the same eye: the shrewdly assessing but always humane eye of both the historian and the poet, each of whom knows that he cannot begin his work until time has passed, revealing the true nature of the object of his contemplation. In both cases, it is the contemplation that redeems that object from oblivion.

Readers encountering these Unfinished Poems will immediately see how fully they partake of Cavafy's special vision, in which desire and history, time and poetry are alchemized into a unified and deeply meaningful whole. Part of the excitement of encountering these Unfinished

Poems for the first time comes, indeed, from the way they seem to fit into the existing corpus, taking their place beside poems that are, by now, well known; there is a deep pleasure in having, unexpectedly, more of what one already loves. But a great deal of the excitement generated by the Unfinished Poems derives, even more, from the new "light," as the poet put it, that they now shed on existing work—on our knowledge of the poet, his techniques, methods, and large ambitions.

Hence a historical figure who until recently seemed to be the object of no more than mild curiosity on the poet's part is now revealed here as the subject of an entire cycle of poems, one that gives us crucial insight into Cavafy's thinking about civilization, ethics, and politics; an unhoped-for trove of new poems about another, already favorite figure includes works that entwine erotic and intellectual preoccupations in new and unexpected ways. (As does a dazzling new poem on a historical subject never before treated by Cavafy, which takes its place beside his very finest work.) One short verse provides the most direct glimpse we get in Cavafy's corpus into the nature of his inspiration; a longer, "philo-sophical" poem reveals that the poet had, in fact, achieved a final, culmi-nating stage in an ethical evolution only now revealed as incomplete in the previously known work. However unfinished these drafts may be, they nonetheless thrillingly round out many aspects of our knowledge of this incomparable artist.

Of these thirty texts, nine treat contemporary subjects that will be familiar to readers already at home in the poet's world. There are evoca-tive treatments of the memory of a deliciously illicit encounter on a wharf ("On the Jetty"), and an elderly poet's reverie about long-past days in which he was a member of a gang of rough young men living at the fringes of society—and on the wrong side of the law ("Crime"). One has as its subject a photograph that elicits thoughts of a bygone love ("The Photograph"); it is a crucial addition to a small but vivid group of poems already known ("That's How," "From the Drawer," "The Ban-daged Shoulder") that indicate how intrigued the poet was by photogra-phy and how suggestively it could figure in his work. A short but vivid lyric, entitled simply "Birth of a Poem," casts a gentle, lunar light on our understanding of the way in which the poet imagined his own creative process to have worked ("imagination, taking / something from life, some very scanty thing / fashions a vision. . . .").

A striking longer work, "Remorse," takes its place beside the most emphatic of Cavafy's philosophical poems—"Hidden Things," "Che Fece . . . Il Gran Rifiuto"—while expanding their moral vision, adding a new note of gentle forgiveness for the unwitting cruelties to which fear and repression condemn us. Surely two of the most remarkable of these poems are "The Item in the Paper," where the melodramatic don-née—a young man is reading an item in a paper about the murder of a youth with whom he'd had a liaison—becomes the vehicle for a tender and devastating exploration of a favorite theme, the soul-destroying effects of taboos against illicit love, and the hypocrisy of those who impose them; and "It Must Have Been the Spirits," a lyric about the noc-turnal revivification of a long-buried past in which, as in some of Cavafy's greatest poems with this motif—"Since Nine—," "Caesarion"—past and present, the quotidian and the intensely erotic, become disori-entingly, thrillingly blurred.

The remaining twenty-one lyrics are historical in nature, although here, as with the best of Cavafy's work, this label is often a matter of convenience. They have familiar Cavafian settings. There are Hellenistic powers teetering—often unbeknownst to the poems' smug narrators—on the brink of implosion ("Antiochus the Cyzicene," "Tigranocerta," "Agelaus," "Nothing About the Lacedaemonians"); the corrupted Egypt of the incestuous Ptolemies ("The Dynasty," "Ptolemy the Benefactor [or Malefactor])"; the Greek-speaking margins of the Roman Empire (the setting of "Among the Groves of the Promenades," the fourth and last of Cavafy's Apollonius of Tyana poems, this one about the sage's sudden, telepathic apprehension, in Ephesus, of Domitian's murder back in Rome). The early Christian era is vividly represented ("Athana-sius," about the Christian bishop who was ill treated by Julian the Apos-tate, a recurring Cavafian character), as are the peripheries of the Greek-speaking world during the twilight of Late Antiquity ("Of the Sixth or Seventh Century"). And of course there is the vast arc of Byzantium, from Justinian (the subject of the spooky short lyric "From the Unpublished History") to the empire's final days.

To the latter epoch, poignant to any Greek, belongs what is surely one of the most striking of any of Cavafy's poems, finished or unfin-ished: "After the Swim," which—as is often the case with the greatest of Cavafy's mature creations—dissolves the distinctions between "historical" and "erotic" poetry, seducing the reader into thinking that the setting is, in fact, that of the late masterpiece "Days of 1908"—a hot Mediterranean day, a seaside swim, naked ephebic bodies—only to reveal, somewhat disorientingly, that we are in the waning days of Byzantium, haunted by the memory of the great scholar Gemistus Plethon, whose own identity (loyally Christian? covertly pagan?) was itself rather vexed.

Of these historical poems, two groups in particular are worthy of special attention because of their immense value to our understanding of the poet's imaginative world. The first is a pair of poems, "The Patriarch" and "On Epiphany," both written in the first half of 1925, whose subject is the fourteenth-century Byzantine ruler John VI Cantacuzenus, "the reluctant emperor"—the regent who felt compelled to take the throne after the foolish widow and conniving ministers of the late emperor, his bosom friend, staged a coup d'état and dragged the empire into a devastating civil war. We know from two Published Poems that date to almost exactly the same period, "John Cantacuzenus Triumphs" and "Of Colored Glass," that this figure evoked a particularly strong emotion in Cavafy, who deeply admired Cantacuzenus's steadfast loyalty, devotion to principle, and—once he had been forced to abdicate, after his enemies' ultimate triumph—great dignity in defeat, along with an impressive piety. The existence of the two Unfinished Poems now makes it clear that during the mid-1920s the poet was hard at work on what amounts to an entire cycle of poems on this poignant and noble figure, a small but significant lyric corpus whose celebration of "the worthiest man whom our race then possessed, / wise, forbearing, patriotic, brave, adroit" sheds greater light on our understanding of the qualities that the mature Cavafy associated with the unique Greek identity for which Byzantium was the conduit. This Cantacuzenus cycle may now take its place alongside the previously known cycles of poems about certain historical figures who similarly evoked a particularly strong response in the poet, not least because of the way their lives shed light on something about what it was to be Greek, or a poet, or both: Marc Antony, Apollonius of Tyana, the apostate emperor Julian.

The other group of historical poems worthy of special note consists, in fact, of no less than four new texts about Julian, now revealed as the figure from the ancient past to whom the poet returned with greatest frequency and intensity: a total of eleven poems in all. (An embryonic twelfth is one of the four fragments in the Cavafy Archive, translated here in the Appendix.) Cavafy's poetic engagement with this complex and enigmatic emperor, who wanted to return the empire to pagan worship not long after it had been converted by his uncle Constantine to Christianity, began early in his creative life, with the Unpublished Poem "Julian at the Mysteries" (1896), and continued virtually to his last days: he had just finished correcting the proofs to "On the Outskirts of Antioch," about Julian's contemptuous treatment of the Antiochene Christians, when he died. The four Unfinished drafts give expression to a wide range of favorite themes and motifs, all clustered around the figure of the emperor, who, in his scheme to impose a dour, humorless, and rigid paganism on the newly Christianized empire, embodied an intolerance, a rigidity of thought, and, worst of all, a profound hypocrisy that to Cavafy represented everything the true Hellenic spirit was not.

And so we have "The Rescue of Julian," with its terse closing reminder, bare of any editorial comment whatever, that the emperor owed his life to the Christian priests he later tormented—a poem that savors of the tart ironies that give works like "Nero's Deadline" their jaundiced effectiveness. "Athanasius," which dramatizes the moment in which two Christian monks in Egypt have a vision of the death of Julian half a world away, in Persia, returns us to the milieu of telepathic perception that had so fascinated the young poet thirty years before. "The Bishop Pegasius," about the still secretly pagan young Julian's encounter with a secretly pagan bishop at an ancient Trojan shrine to Athena, is memorably irradiated by the aura of illicit homosexual attraction that haunts a masterpiece like the Published Poem "He Asked About the Quality." And the perplexed narrator of "Hunc Deorum Templis" must grope in helpless ignorance like the unlucky masses in the early poem "Correspondences According to Baudelaire," which owes so much to the Parnassians' vision of the poet as someone granted a special vision. Contemplating the scene in which, during Julian's triumphant entry into Vienne, an old woman cries out that "here is the man who will restore the [pagan] temples" (the exclamation to which the title refers), this narrator is forced to wonder, rather querulously, whether she is speaking in elation or despair—whether, that is to say, she is a secret pagan sympathizer or a loyal Christian. More secret identities.

The foregoing overview of these rich and quite beautiful works is, of necessity, brief; readers will find a Notes section at the back of this volume designed to provide a detailed historical and literary context for each of the thirty Unfinished Poems. But in sketching the ways in which the present poems partake so richly of the themes and qualities of the poems already well known to us, I hope to have made clear what will, on a close reading of the poems themselves, be evident: that the *Ateli* not only complement our knowledge of the great poet's output, but complete it. The addition of these poems to the canon of Cavafy's published poetry allows us to say, three-quarters of a century after he died on his seventieth birthday—a perfect concentricity, a polished completion—that his work has, at last, been truly finished.

A brief word about the organization of this volume is in order. Renata Lavagnini's Greek edition of the *Ateli* is a work meant for scholars and for Greek-speaking devotees of Cavafy; the present volume must be geared to the needs of the English-speaking reader with no specialized interests, apart from an interest in knowing more about these poems. The Notes therefore assume no special knowledge of Ancient or medieval Greek history, or of poetry in general, apart from that likely to be possessed by any reasonably literate person. I have endeavored to provide commentary that is sufficiently rich for the reader to be able to achieve a full appreciation of each poem in the light of the appropriate background material, whether that material comes from Greek history, or from the world of Cavafy's other poems, or both.

Although much of Professor Lavagnini's edition is, necessarily, devoted to discussions of intricate issues related to textual criticism— material that I have not reproduced in this translation—I suspect that even the casual reader is likely to want to know something about the physical state in which these Unfinished Poems were found. As George Savidis observed in the comment that I cited above, it is clear that the poet carefully organized his work in progress. Each of the poems had its own "dossier." Out of some thick paper—quite often the covers of his own printed collections, which he would appropriate for their new role—Cavafy would fashion a kind of rudimentary envelope (only once did he use an actual envelope), in which he would keep the various bits of paper pertinent to a given poem in progress: drafts, notes, passages from source texts that he had copied out, and so forth. On the outside of the envelope he would write the title (sometimes marked as "provisional") and a date, consisting of the month and year: the moment, as Savidis argues, when Cavafy conceived the poem.

The meticulousness with which the poet conserved his drafts and materials stands, as Professor Lavagnini has noted, in stark and rather amusing contrast to the often quite random nature of his writing materials. These consisted all too obviously of whatever he had to hand at the moment of inspiration—letters that had been addressed to him, invitations to conferences, and, in one memorable case, a scrap of a cigarette box. One thing that this haphazard physical evidence does suggest bears importantly on our understanding of the poet's creative process: clearly, when the moment of inspiration struck, he seized on whatever was immediately available and started writing. Each of my Notes begins with a brief summary, based on the Lavagnini commentary, of the contents of the relevant dossier; I have provided fuller discussion of those contents and the state of the manuscript when I thought such material would be of interest to the general reader.

Many readers are likely to be curious about the physical appearance of the pages themselves, which Professor Lavagnini has rendered accessible through her labors. As is already well known due to the reproduction of some of his manuscripts, Cavafy's handwriting was, generally speaking, forceful and clear (a godsend to the textual critic); he generally wrote in pencil. Divisions between strophes are often clearly marked, as are deletions, which the poet indicated by means of a line through the rejected verses—or, in cases of major deletions, a large wavy line over the entirety of the material to be deleted. Substitutions and additions are written in the space above the original text, and are, in general, made only after the material to be deleted was clearly marked. For this reason, there are relatively few instances in which variant readings appear without any clear indication of what the poet's preference was. (It should, however, be said that in a number of cases, the manuscript pages are somewhat illegible, or show signs of vacillation, with confusingly repeated crossings-out and reinsertions; it is in these cases that Professor Lavagnini's skills as a textual critic have done us the greatest service.)

When there are cases of variant readings in which Professor Lavagnini has been unable to establish priority, I have reproduced these variants (when they are significant, and not merely cases in which the drafts give us one or more synonyms for a given word, as is often the case) in the Notes, with commentary where appropriate. In no case have I chosen to present as part of the translation a variant that has been rejected by Professor Lavagnini. Only in the case of "Epitaph of a Samian" have I deviated from her printed text.*

In the interests of making this volume accessible to the general reader, I am not reproducing what textual scholars refer to as the "diplomatic text"—a text that indicates, by means of a series of conventional notations, all of the additions, deletions, insertions, and emendations that were made at each stage of composition. The texts of the poems themselves in the first part of this volume, therefore, simply reproduce what Professor Lavagnini, with admirable scrupulousness, refers to as "the last" (rather than "the final") of the "forms" that can be construed from Cavafy's manuscript pages. The one exception is that I have reproduced, in the appropriate places in the main text of the poems, the standard notation for illegible characters: a small square cross, each one representing approximately two characters in the original manuscript. It seemed to me that the reader deserves to know where it is simply impossible to make out the poet's intention—an uncertainty, it is worth remembering, that haunts all of these beautiful but unfinished works.

---

*There, I have reproduced as part of the translation itself the added "frame" that Cavafy was struggling to construct without quite being able to reconcile the additional material with the sonnet-form epitaph itself, which he'd written thirty years earlier and was now trying to reconstitute as a more elaborate poem. I have done so in part for practical reasons—to have simply reproduced the sonnet itself, as Professor Lavagnini does in her scholarly text, would have been to present readers with a poem that is already known, the Unpublished "Epitaph" of 1893—and partly because I believe that readers of the present edition will want to see, all at once, what the poet's larger, if never adequately executed, conception for this revamped poem was, a conception that makes the new Unfinished work different from the old poem it sought to transform.

THE
UNFINISHED POEMS

The Item in the Paper

A reference had been made, as well, to blackmail.
And here again the newspaper emphasized
its complete and utter contempt for depraved,
for disgraceful, for corrupted morals.

Contempt . . . And grieving inwardly he
recalled an evening from the year before
which they had spent together, in a room
that was half hotel, half brothel: afterward
they didn't meet again—not even in the street.
Contempt . . . And he recalled the sweet
lips, and the white, the exquisite,
the sublime flesh that he hadn't kissed enough.

Melancholy, on the tram, he read the item.

At eleven at night the corpse was found
on the jetty. It wasn't certain
that it was a crime. The newspaper
expressed its pity, but, as usual,
it displayed its complete contempt
for the depraved way of life of the victim.

It Must Have Been the Spirits

It must have been the spirits that I drank last night,
it must have been that I was drowsing, I'd been tired all day long.

The black wooden column vanished before me,
with the ancient head; and the dining-room door,
and the armchair, the red one; and the little settee.
In their place came a street in Marseille.
And freed now, unabashed, my soul
appeared there once again and moved about,
along with the form of a sensitive, pleasure-bent youth—
the dissolute youth: that too must be said.

It must have been the spirits that I drank last night,
it must have been that I was drowsing, I'd been tired all day long.

My soul was released; the poor thing, it's
always constrained by the weight of the years.

My soul was released and it showed me
a *sympathique* street in Marseille,
with the form of the happy, dissolute youth
who never felt ashamed, not he, certainly.

And Above All Cynegirus

Because he is of a great Italian house,
because he is, also, twenty years of age,
and because this is what they do in the great Greek world,
he came to Smyrna to learn rhetoric,
and to perfect his knowledge of their tongue.

And today he's listening, without
paying any attention at all, to the renowned sophist
who's speaking on Athens; who gesticulates,
and gets carried away, and tells the tale
of Miltiades, and the glorious battle of Marathon.
He's thinking about the drinking party he'll attend tonight;
and his imagination reveals to him a delicate face,
cherished lips that he's impatient to kiss . . .
He's thinking about how well he's doing here.
But his money's running out. And in a few months
he'll be going back to Rome. And he remembers
how many debts he's got there. And that the ordeal
of dodging payments will start all over again,
of finding means to live in a suitable style
(he is of a great Italian house).
Old man Fulvius's will—
ah, if only he could see it. If only he knew
how much he'll be getting from that old bugger

(two years, maybe three; he can't last longer!).
Will he leave him half, a third? It's true
that he's already paid his debts twice before.

The sophist, very deeply moved,
practically in tears, is talking about Cynegirus.

Antiochus the Cyzicene

The people of Syria put up with him:
as long as someone stronger doesn't come along.
And what "Syria"? It barely comes to half;
what with the little kingdoms, with John Hyrcanus,
with the cities that are declaring their independence.

It seems the realm once began, the historians say,
at the Aegean and went right up to India.
From the Aegean right up to India! Patience.
Let's have a look at those puppets,
the animals he's brought us.

On the Jetty

Intoxicating night, in the dark, on the jetty.
And afterward in the little room of the tawdry
hotel—where we gave ourselves completely to our unwholesome
        passion; hour
after hour, again and again to "our own" love—
until the new day glistened on the windowpanes.

This evening the shape of the night resembles,
revived in me, a night of the distant past.

Without any moon, extremely dark
(an advantage). Night of our encounter
on the jetty; at a great
distance from the cafés and the bars.

Athanasius

Inside a boat upon the enormous Nile,
with two faithful monks for his companions,
Athanasius, exiled and harassed
—virtuous, pious, upholding the true faith—
was praying. His enemies were persecuting him
and there was little hope that he'd be saved.
The wind was hard against them;
and their sorry little boat was having trouble making headway.

When he had finished his prayer,
he turned his mournful countenance
toward his companions—and was at a loss
when he saw the curious smile that they had.
While he was at his prayers the monks
had become aware of what was happening
in Mesopotamia; the monks
understood that in that very moment
Julian, that piece of filth, had breathed his last.

The Bishop Pegasius

They entered the exquisite temple of Athena:
the Christian bishop Pegasius
the Christian princeling Julian.
They looked with longing and affection at the statues—
still, they spoke to one another haltingly,
with innuendos, with double-meaning words,
with phrases full of cautiousness,
since neither could be certain of the other
and they were constantly afraid they'd be exposed,
the false Christian bishop Pegasius
the false Christian princeling Julian.

After the Swim

Naked, both of them, as they emerged from the sea at the Samian
shore; from the pleasure of the swim
(a blazing summer's day).
They were slow getting dressed, they were sorry to cover
the beauty of their supple nudity
which harmonized so well with the comeliness of their faces.

Ah the ancient Greeks were men of taste,
to represent the loveliness of youth
absolutely nude.

He wasn't completely wrong, poor old Gemistus
(let Lord Andronicus and the patriarch suspect him if they like),
in wanting us, telling us to become pagan once again.
My faith, the holy one, is always firmly pious—
but you can see what Gemistus was saying, to a point.

On young people at that time the teaching of
Georgius Gemistus had great influence,
who was most wise and exceedingly eloquent;
and an advocate of Hellenic education.

Birth of a Poem

One night when the beautiful light of the moon
poured into my room . . . imagination, taking
something from life: some very scanty thing—
a distant scene, a distant pleasure—
brought a vision all its own of flesh,
a vision all its own to a sensual bed . . .

Ptolemy the Benefactor (or Malefactor)

The poet gave a reading of his poem
which was concerned with the feelings that the campaign
of Agesilaus would likely have provoked in Greece.

Quite obese and sluggish, Ptolemy
the Potbelly—drowsy, too, from overeating—
made an observation: "Learned poet,
these lines of yours are rather overdone.
And the statements about the Greeks precarious, historically speaking."
"Glorious Ptolemy, those are merely trifles."

"Trifles, how? You state explicitly
'The lofty pride of the Greeks . . . the unadulterated
patriotism was awakened. . . .The unchecked rush
to heroism was plain to see among the Greeks.' "

"Glorious Ptolemy, these Greeks,
they are the Greeks of Art, conventional;
bound to feel the way that I do."

Ptolemy was scandalized and opined,
"The Alexandrians are utterly superficial."
Then the poet: "Glorious Ptolemy,
you are the First among the Alexandrians."

"Up to a point," Ptolemy replied, "up to a point.
By birth I'm absolutely undiluted Macedonian.—
Ah, the great Macedonian race, learned poet,
full of derring-do and full of wisdom!"

And heavy as a stone, because he was so fat,
and drowsy from all his overeating
that most undiluted Macedonian
was barely able to keep his eyes open.

The Dynasty

Potbelly's scions. Chickpea, shamefully
expelled from Alexandria, goes to Cyprus. And
Interloper, coming straight from Cyprus,
seizes Alexandria. All of this arranged
by that witch, Scarlet.— The Alexandrians,
who love to chaff, bestowed on them the right
names, without a doubt. More suitable for them are
"Interloper" and "Potbelly" and "Chickpea" and "Scarlet"
than *Ptolemy,* than *Cleopatra.*

From the Unpublished History

Frequently Justinian's gaze
caused terror and revulsion among his servants.
They suspected something that they dared not say:
when by chance one night they were able to confirm
that he was indeed a demon out of Hell:
he came out of his chamber quite late, and went about
headless in the great halls of the palace.

The Rescue of Julian

When the frenzied soldiers slaughtered
Constantine's relations, after he had died,
and finally the dreadful violence
endangered even the little child—six years old—
of the Caesar Julius Constantius,
the Christian priests, compassionate,
found him, and brought him to asylum
in the church. There they rescued him: Julian at the age of six.

Still it's absolutely essential for us to say that
this information comes from a Christian source.
But it's not at all unlikely that it's true.
Historically speaking, there's nothing that seems
incredible: the priests of Christ
rescuing an innocent Christian child.

If it's true—could it be that the very philosophical
Emperor made it clear in this as well, with his
"let there be no memory of that darkness."

The Photograph

Looking at the photograph of a chum of his,
at his beautiful youthful face
(lost forever more;—the photograph
was dated 'Ninety-two),
the sadness of what passes came upon him.
But he draws comfort from the fact that at least
he didn't let—they didn't let any foolish shame
get in the way of their love, or make it ugly.
To the "degenerates," "obscene" of the imbeciles
their sensual sensibility paid no heed.

The Seven Holy Children

How beautifully the Calendar of Saints expresses it:
"Whilst the king spake" with the Saints
"and the Bishops withal and many other nobles,
the Saints did drowse awhile"
and surrendered their souls unto God.

The Seven Holy Children of Ephesus who
escaped into a cave to hide themselves
from the persecutions of the Pagans, and there fell asleep;
and on the morrow woke. Morrow it was for them.
But in the meantime two centuries had passed.

One of them woke on the morrow,
Iamblichus, and he went to buy bread,
and saw before him another Ephesus,
all sanctified with churches, and with crosses.

And the Seven Holy Children rejoiced,
and the Christians honored them and did them reverence;
and from Constantinople came the king,
Theodosius, the son of Arcadius,
and he too reverenced them, as was fitting, that most pious man.

The Seven Holy Children were rejoicing
in this beautiful world, this Christian one,
one sanctified with churches, and with crosses.

But lo, all this was so very different
and they had so much to learn and to say,
(and so powerful a joy can be exhausting, too)
that the Seven Holy Children soon were tired,
coming as they did from another world, from almost two centuries ago,
and in the middle of the conversation they grew drowsy—
and thereupon they closed their saintly eyes.

Among the Groves of the Promenades

Domitian had gone raving mad,
the provinces were suffering dreadfully because of him.
In Ephesus, as elsewhere, despair was great.
When suddenly, one day as Apollonius was speaking
among the groves of the promenades; of a sudden he appeared
to be distracted, to be giving his talk
mechanically. At which point he stopped his talk
and uttered that *strike the tyrant,* in the midst
of his many and extremely puzzled listeners.
In that very moment his soul had seen
Stephanus, in Rome, using his sword to strike
Domitian, who tried to defend himself with a golden goblet
and, finally, the crowds
of spearbearers entering, and straightaway
murdering the vile (and nearly unconscious) king.

The Patriarch

The insolent, the ungrateful John,
who owed the fact that he was Patriarch
to the kindness that was shown to him
by Lord John Cantacuzenus
(the worthy man whom our race then possessed,
wise, forbearing, patriotic, brave, adroit),
played the wise man, the unscrupulous
patriarch did, and said he would take care
that the injustice done long ago to John Lascaris
would never be repeated (not realizing,
silly man, what a tremendous outrage
his words were to the rule of the Paleologues).
Of course he knew, deplorable man, that from
the honorable, the faithful, the unselfish
Lord John Cantacuzenus,
Lord Andronicus's boy was in no danger whatsoever.
He knew it, deplorable, disgraceful man, but sought
in every way to pander to the mob.

On Epiphany

When, at Epiphany, they planned to do the same things once again
that they'd already done at Christmastide,
when they brought their pack of ruffians out once more,
with an eye to dangling, yet again,
the child in front of the people (O alas
for John, the heir to good Lord Andronicus:
who'd have been in better hands with her and her son),

when, at Epiphany, they planned to do the same things once again:
again the vulgar insults of the mob
and the vile innuendoes about her;
she couldn't stand the agony a second time
and in the shabby chamber where she was imprisoned
the Lady Cantacuzene gave up the ghost.

I've drawn the end of Lady Cantacuzene, who died so pitifully,
from the History of Nicephorus Gregoras.
In the historical writings of the emperor
John Cantacuzenus it's treated rather
differently; but not at all less sorrowfully.

Epitaph of a Samian

Stranger, by the Ganges here I lie, a man
who lived a life of lamentation, toil, and pain;
a Samian, I ended in this thrice-barbaric land.
This grave close by the riverbank contains

many woes. Undiluted lust for gold
drove me into this accursed trade.
Shipwrecked on the Indian coast, I was sold
as a slave. Well into old age

I wore myself out, worked until I breathed no more—
deprived of Greek voices, and far from the shore
of Samos. What I suffer now is not, therefore,

fearful; and I voyage down to Hades without grief.
There among compatriots shall I be.
And forever after I shall speak in Greek.

The lines above are taken from the poems,
referring to a time before the Persian Wars,
that Cleonymus the son of Timandrus wrote
in Seleucia, a poet who was patronized
by King Antiochus Epiphanes.

He took a clever pleasure in the jarring phrase:
"Without ever hearing or speaking Greek."

Remorse

Talk about it, this remorse, to soften it—
noble to be sure, but dangerously one-sided.
Don't cling to the past and torment yourself so much.
Don't give so much importance to yourself.
The wrong you did was smaller than you
imagine; much smaller.
The goodness that has brought you this remorse now
was secreted inside you even then.
See how a circumstance that suddenly
returns home to your memory explains
the reason for an action that had hardly seemed
commendable to you, but now is justified.
Don't count too absolutely on your memory;
you've forgotten much—different odds and ends—
that would have justified you quite enough.

And don't presume you knew the man you wronged
so very well. He surely had virtues you were unaware of;
nor perhaps are those deep wounds the ones
that you imagine (out of ignorance of his life)
to be the dreadful blows that came from you.

Don't count on your feeble memory.
Temper your remorse, which is always
so one-sidedly against you, it's casuistry.

The Emperor Conon

Ah goodly patriarch, ah patriarch most righteous,
don't gull yourself with hopes that there can't be
any demolition of the holy icons,
because there's been no sign yet of the emperor Conon.

Ah ill-fated patriarch, don't gull yourself with hopes:
that damnable Leo, look, has come into your room
and now he's going to tell you what his name is.

Hunc Deorum Templis

Blind old woman, were you a secret pagan?
or were you Christian? The words you spoke,
which turned out to be true—that when he made his entrance
into Vienne with all those acclamations, the glorious
Caesar, Julian, was already determined
to serve the sanctuaries of the (false) gods—
the words you spoke, which turned out to be true,
blind old woman: did you speak them in sorrow
as I want to presume or was it, wretched woman, in joy?

Crime

The money was divvied up for us by Stavros.
The best lad in our group,
clever, strong, and beautiful beyond imagining.
The ablest; even though, apart from me
(I was twenty years old), he was the youngest.
I daresay he wasn't quite twenty-three.

Three hundred pounds was the amount that we stole.
He kept, as his fair share, half of it.

But now, at eleven at night, we were planning
how to help him get away tomorrow morning,
before the police found out about the crime.
It wasn't minor: aggravated burglary.

We were inside a cellar.
A basement that was very safe.
Once a plan for his escape had been decided on,
the other three left us, me and Stavros,
with the understanding that they'd come back at five.

There was a tattered mattress on the ground.
Worn out we both collapsed. And what with the emotional
upset, and the weariness,
and the anxiety about his running away

the next day—I barely realized: didn't fully realize
that it was, perhaps, the last time I'd lie near him.

In the papers of a poet this was found.
It does have a date, but it's difficult to read.
The *one* is barely visible; then *nine,* then
one; the fourth number looks like *nine.*

Of the Sixth or Seventh Century

It's very interesting and moving,
the Alexandria of the sixth century, or early in the seventh
before the coming of the mighty Arab nation.
She still speaks Greek, officially;
perhaps without much verve, yet, as is only fitting,
she speaks our language still.
Throughout the Greek world it's destined to fade away;
but here it's still holding up as best it can.

It's not unnatural if we have so feelingly
gazed upon this particular era of hers,
we who now have once more borne
the sound of Greek speech back to her soil.

Tigranocerta

I owe a debt of thanks, I agree,
to my compatriot, one of the family
(my alleged father's cousin: says she)—
that old bawd Kerkó, for telling me
to come here to the brand-new city of Tigranocerta,
so wealthy, blessed in so many ways.

The theater's a way to make my reputation;
I pass quite well as an actor. It isn't
exactly Alexandria here, it isn't Athens.
I was so-so as the Haemon of Sophocles
and so-so as Euripides' Hippolytus.
The spectators said their city had never seen
a more appealing actor—or young man.
A wealthy citizen, fabulously lavish,
took particular note of me.
Kerkó, an old hand, will see to all of that
(taking half for her brokering, the bitch).
Ah, a very special place, Tigranocerta!—
so long as it lasts, that is; since naturally
the Romans will destroy it in the end.
King Tigranes is dreaming.
But what's that to me? At the very most
I'll stay two or three months—then off I go.

At that point I don't give a fig if the Romans destroy
Tigranocerta and Kerkó.

Abandonment

He was far too tasteful and far too clever,
a young man of very good society, too,
to make a fool of himself by acting as if he thought
that his abandonment was some great tragedy.
After all when his friend had said to him, "We two
will have love forever"—both the one who said it,
and the one who heard it, knew it for a cliché.
One night after the picture-show, and the ten
minutes they stayed at the bar, a longing
kindled in their eyes and in their blood
and they went off together, and someone said "forever."

Anyway, their "forever" lasted three years.
Far too often it lasts for less.

He was far too elegant, and far too clever,
to take the matter tragically;
and far too beautiful—both face and body—
for his carnal vanity to be touched at all.

Nothing About the Lacedaemonians

Certainly you ought to love sincerity
and serve it.
Still, don't overdo it, knowing how you'll very likely
reach a point where sincerity won't do.
It's nice; and my, what a splendid feeling.
You'll express yourself honorably and sincerely
on many matters, and you'll be of help.
Rightly they will praise you: what a sincere fellow!
But put some water in your wine: don't presume
since (as you know) "Nothing about the Lacedaemonians."

Zenobia

Now that Zenobia is queen of many great lands,
now that all of Anatolia marvels at her,
and even the Romans fear her by now,
why shouldn't her grandeur be complete?
Why should she be reckoned an Asiatic woman?

They'll make her genealogy straightaway.

See how obviously she's descended from the Lagids.
See how obviously from Macedonia + + .

Company of Four

The money that they make   certainly isn't honest.
But they're clever lads,   these four, and they have found
a way to make it work   and stay clear of the police.
Apart from being cunning,   they are extremely strong.
Because one pair is joined   by the bond of pleasure.
The other two are joined   by the bond of pleasure.
Dressed extremely well   as is fitting for
such good-looking lads;   the theaters and the bars,
and their automobile,   sometimes a little trip—
there's nothing that they lack.

The money that they make   certainly isn't honest:
now and then they fear   that someone will get hurt,
that they might go to jail.   But look, you see how Love
has a power that   can take their filthy money
and make it into something   gleaming, innocent.

Money—none of them   wants it for himself,
wants it selfishly.   None of them counts it out
greedily, boorishly;   they never even notice
if this one's carrying less,   or that one's got a lot.
They share their money out   so that they can be
elegantly dressed,   and spend it lavishly,
so they can make their life   tasteful, as is fitting
for such good-looking lads   so they can help their friends
and then—this is their system—   forget just what they gave.

Agelaus

At the conference of Naupactus Agelaus
said what was only right. Fight no more wars
Greek against Greek. The looming struggle
is drawing nearer to us. Either Carthage
or Rome will be the victor, and afterward
will turn in our direction. O King
Philip, pray consider all the Greeks your own.
If you yearn for wars, prepare yourself
to face whoever's victor over Italy.
It's no longer the time for us to fight each other.
O King Philip, be the savior of Greece.

Words of wisdom. But they weren't heeded.
In the terrible, accursed days
of Cynoscephalae, of Magnesia, of Pydna,
many among the Greeks would recollect
those words of wisdom, which they didn't heed.

NOTES

In these Notes, the date that appears immediately after the title of a poem is the date Cavafy himself wrote on the dossier for that poem—what Savidis calls "the date of first conception." In referring to the dates of composition and/or publication of Cavafy's *Collected Poems*—the Published, Unpublished, and Repudiated Poems—I have followed the system that I adopted in my edition thereof. The year of original composition (and of subsequent rewriting, when known) appears in *italics;* the year (or years) of publication appear in Roman type. Hence, for example, in the case of the Published Poem "Song of Ionia"—of which an early version was written at some point before 1891 and then published in 1896, only to be subsequently revised in 1905 and published in its final form in 1911—the notation reads as follows: "Song of Ionia" (*<1891*; 1896; *1905*; 1911). This, I hope, will allow readers to grasp at a glance the often complicated history of the poems' composition and publication—an evolution that quite often tells us much about the nature of the poet's involvement with and attitude toward a given work.

Words or phrases from the text of a poem that are explained in the Notes—names of people or places, dates, events, etc.—appear in the Note in SMALL CAPITALS.

All translations are my own unless otherwise indicated. Translations of Cavafy's *Notes on Poetics and Ethics* are by Manuel Savidis, with permission gratefully acknowledged herewith.

The Item in the Paper   *pg. 3*

May 1918. The title and date appear on the first of the five sheets comprising the dossier. The relatively large number of papers associated with this poem, and their evidence of many additions, corrections, and revisions, amounting to what Lavagnini has identified as three discrete forms (of which the third is the one reproduced in the main text), offer a particularly intriguing glimpse into Cavafy's creative thinking. The significance of these earlier versions justifies reproducing one of them here—the first, which differs most significantly from the last form. As reconstructed by Lavagnini, it reads as follows:

> He was gloomily reading the item in the papers:
> The crime occurred last night
> around ten. The paper, rightly,
> abhorred the murder, but, typically,
> displayed its complete disdain
> for the reprobate life of the victim,
> for the corrupt individual.
>
> He read. The paper made an error,
> it wouldn't have been ten, but much later.
> They were together until twelve
> (the first time—they barely knew each other
> by sight) in a room that was
> half hotel, half brothel.
> It noted the details of the wound, . . .
> The motive was attempted blackmail . . .
> Mechanically he read about
> the indignation that the reporter felt
> about the crime; and immediately afterward
> about his disdain for the depraved victim.
>
> His disdain. . . . And he, mourning inwardly,
> recalled the sweet lips; the exquisitely
> white, sublime flesh that he hadn't kissed enough.

The second form preserves the basic structure and narrative sequence of the first, adding (after "The paper, rightly / abhorred . . .") the detail that the victim's death was "moreover, an accident, it wasn't intentional": an element that recurs in the last version.

The most important change to both earlier drafts—important for the tone and meaning of the final version, certainly, and also for our appreciation of Cavafy's self-editing—is the displacement, as Lavagnini notes, of the emotionally charged reverie ("His disdain. . . . And he, mourning inwardly, / recalled the sweet lips; the exquisitely / white, sublime flesh that he hadn't kissed enough") from the end of the poem, in the two earlier versions, where it has a more obvious emphatic effect, to the central stanza: a revision that gives the final version greater impact through the imposition of greater restraint.

It Must Have Been the Spirits

pg. 4

February 1919. The first of the six sheets comprising the dossier for this poem gives the title—with a parenthetical indication that it is a temporary title only—along with the date. Sheets 2, 3, and 4 offer evidence of sketches for two discrete early forms; sheet 5 contains the text of the last form, with few corrections, as well as a few lines from the second of the earlier forms. On sheet 6 the poet had written, in English, the word "Superseded," almost certainly referring to the two early sketches.

Here again, evidence for earlier forms provides insight into the process by which the poet made his poem. The task of reconstruction, in this case, was a particularly daunting one, given the number of revisions appearing on each of the sheets and the difficulty of determining a precise order for the verses appearing on them. Lavagnini has constructed the sketches as follows:

Sketch 1 (the text written on sheets 2 and 3) consists of eight lines of a poem that was, at one point, going to feature, prominently it would seem, a mirror:

> The house is closed. No one will be coming tonight;
> Don't shrink back at all, because you'll appear again
> as you were; and the way you are; you haven't changed at all
> Soul of the sensitive, sensual youth—
> of the corrupted youth: of whom, let it be said,
> you'd be ashamed, soul. The house is closed;
> and ten o'clock has come. No one will be coming any more.

> (Far away from the mirror;

Lavagnini has further identified two lines the poet had composed for this poem and later crossed out:

> Don't be bashful [or "draw back"] (neither is the mirror near
>   at hand)
> appear as you were and are: you haven't changed at all.

Lavagnini stresses the significance of the recurrent motif, eventually discarded here, of the mirror as the instrument of (or perhaps inspiration for) the poet's rumination on the past—a device that he would employ, with great success, in the 1930 poem "The Mirror in the Entrance." Here, Cavafy evidently abandoned the mirror motif and turned to another favorite: the sudden, usually nocturnal appearance of ghostly apparitions from the past—either the poet's past or, indeed, the distant past of ancient history. This striking element is a thread that runs consistently through his work: from the earliest phase of his career (in a ghost story he wrote around 1895, "In Broad Daylight," a black-clad male figure appears to a character in the dead of night) through the first decade of the new century (in "January 1904"—the title refers to the date of composition—the poet describes how visions of the past suddenly melt away) and the great production of his middle years. In "Caesarion," for instance, written in 1914 and published four years later, the narrator imagines that he sees the figure of Caesarion, the murdered son of Antony and Cleopatra, in his study, a figure that becomes the vehicle for a reverie at once erotic and historiographical. As the present poem demonstrates, this fascination persisted into the final period of the poet's creative life. For more on this theme, see the note on "Since Nine—" in *Collected Poems*, pp. 399–400.

    Another theme familiar from Cavafy's mature poetry makes itself felt here as well: the way in which memory, and poetry, can be the vehicle for the preservation of a beauty encountered long ago, the physical reality of which will have faded with time. Lavagnini has reconstructed sketch 2 (the text that appears on sheet 4) as follows:

> I don't imagine that he's lived and that he's aged.
> But whatever life has done
> in poetry he's remained just as he was

when I knew him—in a *ruelle*
of Marseille, one happy night
Shape of the sensitive and sensual youth—
of the corrupt youth: that must be mentioned too.

With these we might compare, for instance, these lines from "Days of
1908" (*1921?*; *1932*; *1932*) which exhibit a similar preoccupation:

Oh days of the summer of nineteen-hundred eight . . .
Your vision preserved him
as he was when he undressed, when he flung off
the unworthy clothes, and the mended underwear.

Cavafy had twice spent some time in MARSEILLE. In the early 1870s,
following the premature death of his father, his mother, financially
pressed and hoping to obtain support from her brother-in-law in En-
gland, traveled with her younger sons from Alexandria first to Marseille,
then to Paris, then to London, and finally to Liverpool. The present poem
seems clearly to evoke a memory of the poet's second trip to the port
city—the first stop on the trip to France and England that he took in May
and June 1897, when he was thirty-four, accompanied by his brother
John, who would translate a number of his poems into English. Among
the many souvenirs that the poet saved from this adventure was a handout
from a brothel.

And Above All Cynegirus   *pg. 5*

The first of the three sheets in this poem's dossier gives the title and the
date "July '19." The text of the poem is clean and clear, with few cor-
rections.

The title is a quotation from a work by the satirist Lucian of Samosata
(120–180? A.D.) An accomplished lecturer, essayist, and observer of lit-
erary trends, Lucian was a caustic critic of the Second Sophistic, the
rhetorical movement that flourished between about 60 and 250 A.D.,
and which was marked by a renaissance of interest in the Greek litera-
ture of the high classical period (i.e., the First Sophistic). In his treatise
Teacher of Orators, Lucian is particularly interested in exposing the con-

temporary mania among professional orators and SOPHISTS for aping the Attic style of the great Greek writers of six centuries earlier. Among the archaizing, atticizing clichés that he mocks is the reflexive invocation of the heroism of the Athenian CYNEGIRUS, who died at the battle of Marathon in 490 B.C. In chapter 18 of his treatise, Lucian sarcastically suggests that any would-be orator wishing to make an impression should refer "above all [to] Marathon and Cynegirus."

Cynegirus was the brother of the great playwright Aeschylus; his death, during the rout of the Persians who fled to their ships after the battle (in which the Greeks were led by the general MILTIADES), is graphically recalled in Herodotus's *History* (6.114):

> As the Persians fled, the Greeks followed them, hacking at them, until they came to the sea. Then the Greeks called for fire and laid hold of the ships. At this point of the struggle the polemarch [a senior military officer, Callimachus] was killed, having proved himself a good man and true, and, of the generals, there died Stesilaus, son of Thrasylaus. And Cynegirus, the son of Euphorion, gripped with his hand the poop of one of the ships and had his hand chopped off with an axe and so died, and many renowned Athenians also.

This noble gesture was lovingly recalled by various authors of the Second Sophistic, but there can be little doubt that the one Cavafy had in mind here was M. Antonius Polemo, a sophist who was not only based in Smyrna, as is the unnamed lecturer in this poem, but was also the author of an elaborate display speech about the virtues of Cynegirus, which is extant and would have been available to Cavafy in a number of editions. The speech, which conventionally presents both sides of a debate (this one between the fathers of Cynegirus and Callimachus, as to which son was the greater hero and thus more deserving of receiving a funeral oration), is precisely the kind of grandiose exercise ridiculed by Lucian in his *Teacher of Orators*.

A degree of grandiosity seemed to have been a hallmark of Polemo's personality as well as his style. Born around 88 A.D. to a family of considerable wealth and political attainments, he reached the apogee of his success and influence during the reign of his great patron, Hadrian (ruled 117–138). He served as a representative of Smyrna on important embassies, and tirelessly used his considerable influence to bring greater glory for the city. Known more for his stylistic panache than for any deep intellectual attainments, Polemo was a man of no little swagger even when off the podium; his grandiose habit of traveling in great state and with a considerable retinue trailing behind him provoked the jealous ire of some. That he did not underestimate his own importance to the art of rhetoric was clear. When he was close to death (probably in 144 A.D.), he is said to have asked to be buried alive in the family tomb; while the entrance was being walled up he cried out "Hurry! Hurry! Lest the sun see me reduced to silence!"

Polemo was nonetheless enormously gifted. Widely admired by other sophists, including the great Herodes Atticus (for whom see "Herodes Atticus" in the *Collected Poems,* with note), he was acclaimed for his verbal polish, his penchant for literary allusion—he is said to have endorsed invoking prose authors "by the armful" and poets "by the wagon-load"—and above all for the theatricality of his delivery. This aspect of his professional technique is made much of in the biography of Polemo found in the *Lives of the Sophists* by Philostratus, a work well known to Cavafy, who wrote about it in one of his early articles and indeed used it as a source for other poems, including "Herodes Atticus." In a passage that likely influenced the present poem's reference to the "gesticulations" and excessive emotionality of the sophist lecturing on Cynegirus, Philostratus describes how Polemo, in reaching the climaxes of his arguments, "would jump out of his chair, such was the pitch of excitement that he reached"; at other moments, he would "stamp the ground like the horse in Homer."

Two further elements in Philostratus's text seem to have kindled Cavafy's imagination here. The first is the following description of the students at Polemo's school in Smyrna:

> young people flowed into it from both continents and the islands—nor were they dissolute and promiscuous, but a choice lot and genuinely Hellenic.

The second is an anecdote about a how Polemo got the best of a conceited, spoiled, and vain youth of his acquaintance, who is described as "living a life of dissipation in Smyrna"; although this young man is Ionian, he bears the Roman-sounding name of Varus. It is tempting to think that, coming across these lines, Cavafy might have begun to imagine what a dissolute, promiscuous, and not at all "Hellenic" youth—a real Roman, in fact—might have been daydreaming about while the great orator discoursed about the sterling virtues of the long-dead Athenian hero.

In its dramatic setting, this 1919 poem looks forward to "From the School of the Renowned Philosopher," which was written and published two years later. That poem similarly features a smug young student whose narcissistic daydreams take him far from the world of his master's teachings: as the poem progresses we witness a similar segue from the great world of politics and ambition to the private world of erotic activity:

> He remained Ammonius Saccas's student for two years;
> but of philosophy and of Saccas he grew bored.
>
> Afterward he went into politics.
> But he gave it up. The Prefect was a fool;
> and those around him solemn, pompous stiffs;
> their Greek horribly uncouth, the wretches.
>
> . . . .
>
> Still, he had to do something. He became an habitué
> of the depraved houses of Alexandria,
> of every secret den of debauchery.

The figure of the beautiful young man whose physical allure gives him an inflated sense of himself, a swagger that manages perhaps to be touching even as it irritates, is one to which Cavafy returned in one of the last poems he wrote, "Days of 1908" (*1932; 1935*). Here, the culminating image of the naked boy, godlike in his loveliness, is preceded by an opening description of his contempt for the low-level job he can't bear to hang on to:

> A job, at three pounds a month, at a little stationer's,
> had been offered to him.
> But he turned it down without the slightest hesitation.
> It wouldn't do. It wasn't a wage
> for him, a young man with some education,
> twenty-five years of age.

A variant of the first line makes the Italian boy twenty-two years old, rather than twenty. In almost all of the poet's works focusing on the beauty of appealing young men, the young men in question are in their twenties.

Antiochus the Cyzicene   *pg. 7*

March 1920. The dossier consists of four sheets, the first giving the title and the date. Sheet 2 contains the text for the first stanza, and sheet 3, the text for the second. An alternate title, "Antiochus Grypus" (the epithet means "Hook-nose"), appears above the text on sheet 2. Sheet 4 contains the poet's transcription, with some abbreviations, of a passage about Antiochus the Cyzicene from the ancient historian Diodorus Siculus, from the 1846 Teubner edition (Leipzig).

In this poem Cavafy returns to Syria of the second century B.C., when the mighty Seleucid empire was collapsing—a grand Hellenistic disintegration of the kind that had always fired his imagination, as is evident in such poems as "Orophernes" (*1904*; 1916), "The Seleucid's Displeasure" (*1910*; 1916), and "Demetrius Soter" (*1915*; 1919), and to which he would return at the end of the 1920s in two Published Poems, "Alexander Jannaeus and Alexandra" (*1929*; 1929) and "Should Have Taken the Trouble" (*1930*; 1930). (For a discussion of the history of the Hellenistic monarchies of Macedon, Asia, and Egypt, and their significance in Cavafy's work, see the note in *Collected Poems*, pp. 368–70.) If anything, the short life and career of ANTIOCHUS IX "THE CYZICENE" is an ideal case study both for the fantastically tortured, endlessly

internecine conflicts that plagued the history of the last century of the
Hellenistic Mediterranean, and for the pathetic inadequacy of the later
Hellenistic monarchs to live up to the grandeur of their legacy from
Alexander and his generals—a favorite theme to which Cavafy returns
in other Unfinished Poems, as witness the present poem, "Ptolemy the
Benefactor (or Malefactor)," and "The Dynasty."

Antiochus was born around 137 B.C. to the Seleucid emperor Anti-
ochus VII and his wife, Cleopatra Thea, a daughter of Ptolemy VI of
Egypt whose extravagant marital career had included prior marriages
first to the pretender Alexander Balas (see "Demetrius Soter (1915;
1919) and "Favour of Alexander Balas" (1916?; 1921), and then Anti-
ochus VII's brother, Demetrius II. Antiochus IX was called "the Cyz-
icene" because upon his father's death in 129, when his uncle Demetrius
reclaimed the throne, his mother sent him for safekeeping in Cyzicus, a
city on the Sea of Marmara. After Demetrius II's death in 126, his son by
Cleopatra Thea, Antiochus VIII Grypus ("Hook-nose")—which is to say,
Antiochus the Cyzicene's half brother—assumed the throne jointly with
his mother: a step that was taken, it should be noted, only after she had
killed her other son by Demetrius, the ill-named Seleucus V Philomator
("Mother-loving"). Inevitably, a civil war broke out between the two
brothers, although eventually the two divided the kingdom between
them, a move that only contributed to the disintegration of the once-
great Seleucid realm.

As a result of the power vacuum created by civil war, many Syrian
cities declared themselves independent, and ambitious strongmen
throughout the region made themselves monarchs of short-lived king-
doms. The ongoing chaos in Syria—which had formerly controlled
Judea with an iron grip—inevitably furthered the political aims of men
such as the Judean aristocrat JOHN HYRCANUS, a son of the high priest
and freedom fighter Simon Maccabee (brother of Judah), and the father
of Alexander Jannaeus (see "Alexander Jannaeus" in Collected Poems). In
particular, Hyrcanus took advantage of the unstable reign of Demetrius
II to overrun and raze Samaria and to invade Idumaea (the Edom of the
Hebrew Bible).

As he often like to do, Cavafy derived his poem from two sources,
one ancient and one modern. The latter was A. Bouché-Leclercq's His-

toire des Seleucides (323–64 avant J. C.) (Paris, 1913–1914), which in turn uses an anecdote about the monarch that occurs in the text of the first-century B.C. historian Diodorus of Sicily (ca. 90–30 B.C.). (Diodorus's *Historical Library,* liberally culled from the works of other historians and originally published in forty books—of which fifteen have survived—sought to trace the history of the world from the Trojan War through the middle of the first century B.C.; which is to say, the historian's own time.) In the passage that Cavafy copied out onto the fourth of the sheets in the dossier for the present poem, taken from the thirty-fifth book of Diodorus's work, the ancient historian comments, not without sarcasm, on Antiochus's insatiable love of amusement, particularly the-atricals of all sorts:

> Once he had gained the throne, Antiochus the Cyzicene fell into habits of drunkenness and luxurious excess and enthusi-asms utterly inappropriate to a king. He took great pleasure in mimes and pantomime performers and all sorts of show people, and he eagerly devoted himself to learning their var-ious crafts. And he took up puppetry as well; and so learned to maneuver silver-plated and gilded animal figures five cubits high, and many other such devices. But he did not pos-sess any "city-takers" or other machinery for besieging cities, which might have brought him great glory, and would have been a distinction that was actually worthy of note. He was immoderately fond of hunting at odd hours, and often, at night, keeping it a secret from his intimates, he would slip out into the countryside with two or three of the household and would hunt lion and panther and wild boar. And in grap-pling so closely with savage beasts he often put himself in the very greatest danger.

The strange and distinctive collocation of high-stakes international political gamesmanship and ostensibly innocuous theatrical entertain-ments—the idea of a king who is also merely a "player"—clearly appealed to the poet, with his strong sense of the foibles that lay beneath royal pretensions: see, for instance, "King Demetrius" (*1900; 1906*).

On the Jetty *pg. 8*

April 1920. The dossier consists of only two sheets, the first bearing the title and the date, the second containing the text of the poem, written with some haste and often difficult to make out.

The following variant readings are worth noting; the last one, an alternate for the final line, indicates that Cavafy had at some point completely revised his idea for the setting of this poem.

LINE 3   where we gave ourselves completely to our
            unwholesome, beautiful passion

OR   when we had had our fill of lovemaking

LINE 4   again and again to our own love

LINE 5   until the new day glistened on the windowpanes

LINE 10–11   in the park, at a great distance
            from the houses and the carriages and the trams.

The setting of the jetty as a site for illicit erotic meetings links this poem to the earliest of the Unfinished drafts, "The Item in the Paper."

Athanasius *pg. 9*

April 1920. Four sheets, the first bearing the title and the date. Sheet 2 contains the text of the poem; sheet 3 features the poet's transcription of his source material (a passage from E. L. Butcher's *Story of the Church of Egypt*); sheet 4, a variant reading of the final three lines, along with a note by the poet indicating that he had not successfully located the source of Butcher's story.

ATHANASIUS, bishop of Alexandria (ca. 295–373), was a vigorous leader of the Egyptian church during the ideologically and politically turbulent fourth century; among other things, he was a great scholar of the concept of the Incarnation and an implacable foe of the hugely controversial Arian heresy (named for the Alexandrian priest Arius [250–336], who insisted that the person of Jesus was not consubstantial or coeternal with God the Father, a position that set him at odds with the

Nicene Creed). Born in Alexandria, Athanasius was ordained by the Alexandrian patriarch, Alexander, when he was in his early twenties, and likely served as Alexander's secretary at the Council of Nicaea in 325. He succeeded Alexander as patriarch in 328, despite his extreme youth and, even more, despite strong opposition from Arius and his supporters, some of whom were powerful bishops, such as Eusebius of Nicomedia.

Conflict with the Arian faction was to plague Athanasius throughout his reign—one that was, too, intricately bound up with the tumultuous imperial politics of the era of Constantine the Great and his successors. In 335 he was deposed by an Arian cabal and later on, having been rather fancifully accused by his enemies of interfering with the Egyptian grain supply, he was banished to the Rhineland by the emperor Constantine. On Constantine's death in 337 he returned to Alexandria, only to be banished once again the following year by the late emperor's son, Constantius II, who was an Arian. (Indeed, after Constantius slaughtered most of the family of his young cousin Julian during the dynastic power struggle precipitated by Constantine's death—the subject of the Unfinished Poem "The Rescue of Julian"—he insisted on an Arian religious education for Julian, whose teacher was none other than Eusebius of Nicomedia.) Athanasius returned again to Alexandria in 347 with the backing of Constantius's brother and co-emperor Constans, who was based in Rome, but he was banished yet again on the death of Constans, in 350.

During these upheavals he managed to write powerful treatises against Arianism, in one of which, perhaps understandably, he likens Constantius to the Antichrist. (He also composed his *Life of Saint Anthony,* which proved enormously influential on the development of the Christian hagiography.) It was on Constantius's death in 361 that Athanasius, who by this time had become something of a folk hero in Egypt, was allowed at last to return once more to Alexandria under an amnesty granted by the new emperor, Julian the Apostate, to exiled bishops; no doubt his experience of the preceding years informed the impassioned call for Christian unity that he issued on his return to his native city. In the next year, however, Julian, who was bitterly disappointed in his hopes that Athanasius would foster dissension among the Christian factions, had Athanasius banished from Alexandria to Upper

Egypt. (A detailed note on Julian's life and career and their significance for Cavafy's work can be found in *Collected Poems,* pp. 360–3.)

Until Julian's death in battle in 363, Athanasius often lived in fear for his life; it is in this period that the present poem is set. As is already clear from his several poems about Apollonius of Tyana (for instance, the Published Poems "But Wise Men Apprehend What Is Imminent" and "If Indeed He Died," or the Unfinished Poem "Among the Groves of the Promenades"), incidents of supernatural perception on the part of profoundly gifted or spiritual men exerted a particular fascination on Cavafy, and we may add the present poem to what constitutes a kind of cycle of poetic explorations of this abstruse supernatural theme. (Apollonius, in fact, exemplified the literary type of the supernaturally gifted miracle worker, which influenced Athanasius's depiction of St. Anthony in the *Life.*) Cavafy's original source material for this poem was a passage from Butcher's *Story of the Church of Egypt* (1895), which he transcribed onto one of the sheets that make up the dossier for this poem:

> Athanasius stayed some time in Hermopolis and Antinoë, preaching and openly performing his duties, as if on an ordinary visitation tour; but at midsummer he received fresh warning that he was in danger, and Theodore came again with another abbot to entreat him to conceal himself in Tabenna. He embarked in a covered boat with the 2 monks; but the wind was against them, and it became necessary to tow the boat with painful slowness. Athanasius was for some time absorbed in prayer, and did not observe the faces of his two companions. At length he turned to them and began "If I am killed"—but broke off as a curious smile passed between the two monks, who thereupon informed him that even while he prayed they had received a supernatural intimation that Julian was no more. Julian was, in fact, slain on the field of battle on June 26, 363.

A note, dated November 1929 and attached as the fourth sheet in the dossier for this poem, suggests the impressive scholarly rigor characteristic of Cavafy's method. In it, the poet indicates that over the course of the decade since the composition of this poem, he had attempted, and failed, to find a primary source for Butcher's colorful anecdote in J. P. Migne's *Patrologia Graeca,* an immense mid-nineteenth-century collection of the Greek writings of the Church Fathers. The note ends with the poet's instruction that if the story found in Butcher could not be authenticated by a primary source, the poem "could not stand." The scholar Glen Bowersock has since completed the poet's work, locating the source of the story in *Patrologia Graeca* (volume 26, columns 980C–81C).

A variant to the last line reads as follows:

> . . . what was happening in Mesopotamia.
> The vile Julian, in that very moment,
> The vile Julian had ceased to live.

The Bishop Pegasius pg. 10

May 1920. Cavafy wrote the date on the covering sheet for this dossier of five sheets, which also bears the title, one of the two he considered for this poem. The text of the poem appears on sheet 2 (on the back of which are written the two titles: "The Bishop Pegasius" and "The Temple of Athena"), with a few lines and words appearing as well on sheet 3. Sheets 4 and 5 contain references to and citations from sources for the incident described in the poem.

The poem refers to an event that took place in the autumn of 355. En route to see his uncle, the emperor Constantius, in Mediolanum (that is, Milan, where Constantius would bestow on him the title of *caesar* on November 6, 355), the twenty-one-year-old Julian took time to visit the city of Ilion, near the coast of Asia Minor—the site of the ancient city of Troy. After he had become emperor and begun his work of restoring pagan worship, Julian addressed a letter to a pagan priest, dating perhaps to 362, in which the emperor defends a certain pagan called PEGASIUS (who, a former Christian bishop, had had his pagan bona fides questioned). Julian describes how he had been taken to see the ancient temples by Pegasius when the latter was bishop of Ilion, and how the two men, both secretly pagan, had subtly tested each other:

> Pegasius came to meet me, and as I wanted to explore the city—for this was my pretext for visiting the shrines—he became my guide and took me round everywhere. Listen now to his deeds and words, from which you might reckon that he did not lack the proper attitude toward the [pagan] gods.
>
> There is a hero's shrine of Hector where a bronze statue of him stands in a little temple. Opposite this, they've set up a great figure of Achilles, in the unroofed courtyard. If you've seen the place, you'd recognize it from my description. . . . Finding that the altars were still lighted, indeed one might say ablaze, and the statue of Hector had been anointed till it gleamed, I said, with a look at Pegasius, "What's this, then? Do the people of Ilion offer sacrifices?"— carefully probing him to see what his thoughts were. And he replied, "And what's unusual in worshiping a brave man, one of their own countrymen, just as we worship our martyrs?" The comparison was hardly sound; but judged by the standards of those times, his opinion was a cultured one. And the rest? "Let us proceed now," he said, "to the temple of Athena of Ilion." After which he took me there with the greatest eagerness and opened up the temple and, like someone producing a piece of evidence, showed me all the statues in perfect condition, nor did he do any of the things that impious men were wont to do, tracing the sign [of the cross] on their foreheads; nor did he whistle, as such men would do, to himself. For those two things are the height of their theology, whistling at spirits and making the sign of the cross on their foreheads.

Julian goes on to note that although it was true that Pegasius, while bishop, had done some damage to some of the gods' temples, this was merely a blind, to throw off those who might suspect his secret paganism. This elaborately contrived secrecy, betraying as it did a terror of being exposed, together with the cautious, probing phrases, the double entendres and veiled allusions, inevitably recall the charged atmosphere of secret homosexual encounters familiar from poems that have a contemporary setting, such as "In the Window of the Tobacco Shop" (*1907*; 1917) and "He Asked About the Quality" (*1930*; 1930).

Ten years after he began work on this poem, Cavafy was evidently still pondering the fraught encounter between the secretly pagan prince and the secretly pagan bishop. Among the notes in the dossier for this poem there is a lengthy citation of a description of the Julian-Pegasius encounter by the French historian Joseph Bidez, whose *La Vie de L'Empereur Julien* was not published until 1930, fully ten years after the poet had penned this draft.

The word I have translated as "princeling" in line 3 is *igemoniskos,* a diminutive of *igemonas* (related to the English *hegemon*), meaning "ruler" or "potentate"; the diminutive has a certain contemptuous force. A variant for this line describes Julian as *prinkips,* which is a Greek transliteration of the Latin *princeps,* and is a more neutral way of referring to a member of the imperial household. A variant to the fourth line reads as follows:

> upon the ruin of the pagan rite
> they looked with deep emotion

After the Swim

pg. 11

June 1921. The covering sheet, bearing the date and the title, includes a note indicating that Cavafy considered the title to be provisional. Sheet 2 contains the text of the first three stanzas, and sheet 3 the text of the final stanza, along with material related to the earlier stanzas, including the variant for line 4.

This remarkable poem rather startlingly unites a shimmering eroticism with an equally charged, almost yearning evocation of the last days of Byzantium. Always in Cavafy's evocations of Byzantium—the civilization that for Greeks such as the poet represented a cultural conduit linking ancient times to the present day—there is a quality of wistful yearning, which, as the scholar Diana Haas noted, is often represented by the emotionally charged use of the possessive pronoun "our" when speaking of the Byzantine culture or its people. We find it, for instance, in "In the Church" (*1892*; *1901*; *1906*; *1912*?), where he has the striking phrase *o endoxos mas Vizantinismos,* "our glorious Byzantinism," or in the 1914 Unpublished Poem "Theophilus Palaeologus," where the possessive pronoun is explicitly linked to the word for "yearning," *kaïmos,* in the phrase *poson kaïmo tou yenous mas,* "how great a yearning of our race." The special kind of longing that contemplation of Byzantine civilization inspired in Cavafy—rich yet exhausted, glorious yet doomed, proudly attempting to uphold great traditions even as it disintegrates—is made concrete in the present text in the almost voyeuristic appreciation of the lissome beauty of the youths coming from their swim; that erotic yearning is then explicitly linked to Byzantium by the revelation that the young men are, in fact, students of the great Byzantine scholar GEORGIUS GEMISTUS PLETHON.

Gemistus (ca. 1355–1452) was a leading Neoplatonist, a principal figure in the revival of Classical learning in Western Europe and a man of remarkably broad learning and curiosity. Although he taught philosophy at Constantinople, he studied Zoroastrianism and other abstruse teachings with the Jewish scholar Eliseus. A rare champion of the Platonic (as opposed to the far more prevalent Aristotelian) philosophical vision, he is said to have taken the additional surname *Plêthon,* an archaizing synonym for *gemistos,* "full," because it sounded like "Plato." He was the author of, among other works, a tract on the differences between Plato and Aristotle, and a pamphlet urging Manuel II Palaeologus (a son of the emperor, John VIII, and the ruler of the Peloponnesian province of Morea) to reorganize the social structure of the Morea along the lines of Plato's *Republic.* This grandiose vision of an application of Classical philosophical principles to real life moved Paparrigopoulos, the nineteenth-century historian of Greek culture so important to the poet, to compare Gemistus to a figure of particular interest to Cavafy: Julian. "The man," Paparrigopoulos wrote, "seems to have fallen into the error of Julian the Apostate, and on behalf of this doctrine maintained beliefs inimical to Christianity"—a comparison of which the poet, always alert to anything to do with Julian, is sure to have taken note.

It was, indeed, Gemistus Plethon's particular preference for Plato, perceived as a covert paganism, that aroused the ire of church authorities. Eventually his Aristotelian rival, Georgios Scholarios (who later, as Gennadius II, would become the first PATRIARCH of Constantinople after the city fell to the Ottomans in 1453), persuaded the emperor Manuel II Palaeologus to exile Gemistus to the fortress-city of Mistras in the Peloponnese on suspicion of heresy; the order may have been carried out by Manuel's son, ANDRONICUS. In his final work, the *Book of Laws,* an attempt to synthesize Neoplatonism and belief in the Olympian gods, the elderly Gemistus flatly stated that Zeus was the supreme god. The treatise was burned by Scholarios.

Gemistus's extraordinary influence on the rebirth of interest in Plato in Western Europe stems from his early association with the emperor John VIII Palaeologus, whom he accompanied as a delegate to the Councils of Ferrara in 1438 and of Florence in 1439, which were devoted to discussions of a reunion of the Western and Eastern Churches. It was during this stay in Italy that Gemistus gave lectures on Plato to interested Italians, thereby reintroducing Platonic thought to a Europe that had been familiar primarily with Aristotle. The influence of his teachings in Florence was so great that Cosimo de' Medici was inspired to found the Accademia Platonica, whose first director referred to Gemistus as "the second Plato." (The fall of Constantinople in the year following Gemistus's death furthered the renaissance of Classical learning in Western Europe, as Byzantine scholars sought refuge in the West.) Gibbon, in his description of Gemistus's activities in Italy, has nothing but admiration for his "sublime thoughts": "sometimes adapted to familiar conversation, and sometimes adorned with the richest colours of poetry and eloquence."

Two alternate readings are worth noting because they suggest the extent to which Cavafy was debating how much to emphasize the erotic elements in this poem, which so unexpectedly reveals itself as a "historical" poem. For lines 4–5 Lavagnini notes the following variant:

> They were slow to get dressed, taking pleasure as they did
> in the sight of the flesh of their desirable limbs.

This variant suggests quite strongly the physical reality of the erotic desire in question; in this variant we find, too, the important Cavafian word *idoni,* "pleasure" (in the verb <u>*idoni*</u>*zomeni,* "taking pleasure"). The aesthetic and erotic resonances of this scene—the naked youths, the emphasis on the beauty of limbs freed of the constraints of clothing at the seaside bathing spot—powerfully recall the final stanza of the Published Poem "Days of 1908," with its narrator's reverie about a working-class youth:

> Your vision preserved him
> as he was when he undressed, when he flung off
>   the unworthy clothes, and the mended underwear.
> And he'd be left completely nude; flawlessly beautiful;
>   a thing of wonder.
> His hair uncombed, springing back;
> his limbs a little colored by the sun
> from his nakedness in the morning at the baths,
>   and at the seashore.

In her important study of the problems of religion in Cavafy's early work (*Le problème religieux dans l'oeuvre de Cavafy: Les Années de formation [1882–1905]*, Sorbonne, 1996), Diana Haas has offered the intriguing suggestion that one reason Cavafy might have laid this draft aside without finishing it was that a mere month after its composition, in July 1921, he began work on an early version of "Days of 1908," which bore the title "The Summer of 1895" and may have expressed more directly the themes with which he was preoccupied at that moment, which seem ultimately to have been more erotic than historical.

In this context it is particularly interesting to note that, in an earlier form of the last line, the poet had described Gemistus first as a "lover," *erastis,* of "Hellenic letters," only to cross out that line and replace it with "an admirer of the Greek's way of life," which he subsequently deleted in favor of the last form, reproduced here.

Birth of a Poem   *pg. 12*

February 1922. Of the two sheets in this folder, one bears the title and the date; the second contains the text of the poem, the title "Birth of a Poem," and an alternate title, "A Vision All Its Own."

Lavagnini observes a connection between this poem and "In a Town of Osrhoene" (*1916*; *1917*), in which an apparition revealed by moonlight is the spur to strong emotion:

> From the tavern brawl they brought him back to us, wounded—
> our friend Rhemon, around midnight yesterday.
> Through the windows we'd left open all the way
> the moon illumined his beautiful body on the bed.
> We're a hodgepodge here: Syrians, Greeks, Armenians, Medes.
> Rhemon is one, too. But yesterday, as the moon
> shone on his sensuous face
> we were put in mind of Plato's Charmides.

If that poem links moonlight to a concrete instantiation of beauty, another poem that Cavafy saw fit to publish in *1917*, "I've Gazed So Much" (*1911*, *1917*), looks forward to the present poem in the way it connects corporeal loveliness recalled at nighttime to the inspiration for, and requirements of, poetic art:

> At beauty I've gazed so much
> that my vision is filled with it.
>
> The body's lines. Red lips. Limbs made for pleasure.
> Hair as if it were taken from Greek statues:
> always lovely, even when it's uncombed,
> and falls, a bit, upon the gleaming brow.
> Faces of love, exactly as
> my poetry wanted it . . . in the nights of my youth,
> secretly encountered in my nights.

There is a variant reading of line 4, crossed out on the manuscript:

> the faint occasion for a distant scene

Ptolemy the Benefactor (or Malefactor) *pg. 13*

February 1922. The dossier for this poem contains nine sheets, in which Lavagnini has detected fully five versions of the poem, three of which with significant variants (reproduced below).

PTOLEMY VIII (182–181 to 116 B.C.; he is sometimes numbered VII, the numbering of the incestuous and parricidal Ptolemies being notoriously problematic), the son of Ptolemy V and Cleopatra I, gave himself the grandiose epithets Euergetes ("BENEFACTOR") and Tryphon ("Magnificent"); the Alexandrians, famous for their sardonic wit, redubbed him "Kakergetes" ("MALEFACTOR") and, because of his notorious girth, "Physkon" ("POTBELLY").

From his earliest youth, Ptolemy VIII was in conflict with his older brother, Ptolemy VI (186–145 B.C.), who bore the conventional epithet Philomator ("Mother-loving") because he ascended the throne at the age of six with his mother as co-ruler of the Lagid house of Egypt. (This Ptolemy VI was the father of Cleopatra Thea, mother of Antiochus IX of Syria, the subject of the Unfinished Poem "Antiochus the Cyzicene.") In 164 B.C., after he was expelled from Alexandria by his ambitious younger sibling, the elder Ptolemy appealed to Rome for assistance in winning back his throne: this is the incident to which the Published Poem "Envoys from Alexandria" alludes. The Romans backed the elder brother, dispatching the younger to rule Cyrene in North Africa; but after the elder brother's death in 145, the younger returned to Alexandria as Ptolemy VIII. In the following year he married his brother's widow, Cleopatra II, who was also the sister of both men. Almost immediately he killed her son by Ptolemy VI (the boy is sometimes referred to as Ptolemy VII), and two years after his succession he married her daughter by Ptolemy VI, Cleopatra III. By Cleopatra III, who was both his stepdaughter and niece, he fathered Ptolemy IX and Ptolemy X, brothers whose internecine rivalry in many ways replicated that between their father and uncle (see the Unfinished Poem "The Dynasty").

Even by the decayed standards of the later Ptolemies, Ptolemy VIII Euergetes stands out as having been particularly loathsome: according to all reliable sources he was physically repellent (contemporary Greeks were horrified that the obese monarch favored the transparent garments of the Egyptians, rather than the modestly opaque dress of the

Greeks), paranoid, and murderously cruel. He seems to have been particularly vindictive against those whom he saw as supporters of his late older brother, Ptolemy VI. These groups included Alexandria's Jews (whom, according to the historian Josephus, the king tried to have trampled by elephants: an incident that the biblical book of Maccabees assigns to an earlier Ptolemy) and particularly the city's thriving intellectual class, many of whom, as a result of Ptolemy's persecutions, fled Alexandria and scattered throughout the Mediterranean.

And yet despite his oppression of the Alexandrian intelligentsia, Ptolemy was not without considerable intellectual pretensions himself. He was a pupil of the great literary scholar Aristarchus, the head of the Alexandrian library (which the king supported), and is said to have delighted in abstruse literary debate of the kind which Cavafy evokes in the present poem. He left no fewer than twenty-four volumes of memoirs.

The interpretation of the present poem stems from a proper understanding of the subject of the discussion between the belletrist monarch and the fictional court poet, who has evidently composed a work on a bit of history already three hundred years old at the dramatic date of the poem: the Asian campaign of the Spartan king and general AGESILAUS II (444–360 B.C.). Already middle-aged by the end of the Peloponnesian War, which saw the defeat of Athens and the triumph of Sparta, Agesilaus—who was lame and rumored to be the son of the aristocratic Athenian statesman Alcibiades—led a force of eight thousand allied troops into Asia in 396, in order to guarantee the safety of the coastal Greek cities, an expedition he rather grandiosely saw as a modern-day Trojan War. To underscore the parallel, he sought to offer a sacrifice at Aulis prior to sailing for Asia, as the Greek forces did in the legend of the Trojan War; but the Theban allies objected, thereby winning Agesilaus's undying enmity.

Once in Asia, however, Agesilaus is said to have begun entertaining the idea of a far grander project: a campaign into the Asian interior and an attack on the Persian king Artaxerxes II. Before he was able to undertake this enterprise, however, he was recalled to Greece due to the explosion of hostilities between Sparta and a coalition of Greek city-states including Athens, Corinth, Thebes, and Argos. Although he was successful in some of his encounters with the anti-Spartan coalition, the Spartan fleet under his leadership suffered a devastating defeat at sea at the hands of the Persians (whose leadership included the Athenian admiral Conon, only too happy to have a chance to revenge himself on the Spartans after the cataclysmic Athenian defeat in the Peloponnesian War).

A detail from Paparrigopoulos's account of Agesilaus's Asian campaign suggests why the fourth-century Spartan king's expedition sparked Cavafy's imagination—and why he chose to frame it in a late Ptolemaic, second-century B.C. context. For the nineteenth-century Greek historian so greatly favored by Cavafy describes Agesilaus as "the true forerunner of Philip and Alexander"; which is to say, the Macedonian kings Alexander the Great, who successfully invaded Asia and toppled the Persian empire in the 330s B.C., and his father, Philip II, whose idea the Asian campaign originally had been. Alexander's conquests, of course, created the Hellenistic world that is the setting of this poem: as we know, following his death and the breakup of his world empire, his general Ptolemy became the pharaoh of Egypt, and was therefore the source of the Macedonian blood of which his distant, decadent descendant, Ptolemy Physkon, here rather preposterously boasts.

Another irony suggested by the invocation of Agesilaus (in light of Paparrigopoulos's phrasing) is that "the feelings that the campaign of Agesilaus would likely have provoked in Greece" were, if anything, the opposite of the "lofty pride" and "unchecked rush to heroism" that the ignorant poet rather optimistically imagines. For the Asian campaigns of both Alexander and his "forerunner," Agesilaus, provoked hostility and suspicion among the other Greek states; as we know, Agesilaus was unable to undertake his planned invasion precisely because the Greeks back home were rising against Sparta. Cavafy, then—the "poet-historian" whose own historical method was so rigorously scholarly and meticulous—presents here a poet who is grossly ignorant of history; while, in a further irony, the "Macedonian" who does know his history— Ptolemy himself—is so clearly an unworthy successor to the illustrious ancestor whose name he bears, and who was a proud participant in that earlier Asian campaign.

The evolution of this poem from its earliest to its last extant version suggests a typically rigorous self-editing on Cavafy's part. As the poem took shape, he stripped away a good deal of material about Ptolemy's knowledge of history, which in the later version is merely inferred; and he also removed references to further details of the history of Agesilaus's expedition (the sacrifice at Aulis, for instance). The result is a poem at once more evocative and more pointed.

The first version contains the following two passages:

> The poet gave a reading of many excerpts—
> in a pleasant voice, with a sweet delivery—
> of his work
> about the expedition of Agesilaus;
> and the grandees showered him with praise.
> Ptolemy —— —— —— ——
> —— —— —— —— —— —— ——
>
> listened too, attentively.
> It happened that he had some vague knowledge
> about the subject, mostly schoolboy
> recollections of the history of the Greeks
> from the conscientious studies of his youth.

And, from Ptolemy's address to the poet:

> Learned poet, your verses are quite good:
> but historically quite without foundation.
> +++ that the Thebans, while at Aulis,
> wouldn't even permit the sacrifice.
> Conon armed the Persian fleet.
> And a coalition of Thebans, Corinthians, and Athenians
> put an end to the expedition of Agesilaus.

The second and third versions do not vary significantly, but the fourth version—far lengthier than the final version—is the longest, and very rich in material that the poet later excised:

> The poet (certainly not received at the Museum,
> certainly not renowned through all of Greece
> but someone rather well-liked at Court)

was reciting before Ptolemy the king
lengthy excerpts from his poem about
the expedition of Agesilaus.
The king and the courtiers applauded him warmly.
Afterward, Ptolemy said: "Learned poet,
your verses are lovely, but it seems to me
that you've been lax about the historical truth.
You've represented us Greeks as being of one mind.
You forget the Thebans, and the snub that they
offered to your hero while at Aulis.
As for the Athenians, you've forgotten that . . .
And what Conon did to him at sea.
Maybe not as well as you, wise poet, but still—
we know a bit of Greek history ourselves."
"Glorious Ptolemy, all that is immaterial."
"Immaterial how? You put it quite explicitly.
You say 'the Greeks were galvanized' and elsewhere,
if I heard aright, 'all of Greece'
and elsewhere again that 'all the Greeks eagerly dashed off.' "
"Glorious Ptolemy, those Greeks
are the Greeks of Verse, symbolic:
and they feel just what I decide they should."
Ptolemy was puzzled and he murmured
"The Alexandrians are really quite superficial."
"Glorious Ptolemy," said the poet,
"of the Alexandrians You are the foremost."
"Undoubtedly," Ptolemy replied, "undoubtedly. But
my stock is of the purest Macedonian.
Ah, a remarkable people, the Macedonians, Learned Poet,
full of derring-do and full of wisdom."
And seeing that, because of his great slothfulness
and his girth, the smallest step would be an awful problem,
and because of his obesity, that pile of flesh,
and sleepy from his overeating and excessive drinking
he who was of the purest Macedonian
was barely able to keep his eyes open.

In its evocation of the fraught relationship between a court poet and his royal patron; in the way in which an evocation of earlier Greek history casts a bitterly ironic light on a later, corrupted age; and in particular in its subtle but pointed allusion to a historical episode involving a Greek invasion of Asia, the present poem, dated February 1922, strongly recalls the Published Poem "Darius" (*1897?*; *1917*; *1920*). And it is surely worth considering both poems, and indeed other poems of the early and mid-1920s, particularly the John Cantacuzenus cycle (for which see the notes on "The Patriarch" and "On Epiphany," pp. 77–82 and 82–7), in the light of the Greco-Turkish War of 1919–1922—a modern-day example of a disastrously ill-conceived and ill-executed Greek invasion of Asia. The war arose out of the irredentist concept of the *Megali Idea* or "Great Idea," the longstanding nationalist Greek dream (and a cornerstone of foreign policy almost since the establishment of the independent Greek state in the 1820s) of a "Greater Greece" encompassing large Greek Christian communities, such as that in Izmir (Smyrna), still living under Turkish domination in Asia Minor. The war began with a massive Greek landing at Izmir, and at first went well for the Greeks; but as Turkish resistance stiffened, the tide began to turn. The years 1921 and 1922 saw reverses for the Greeks, starting in the interior and moving toward the coast, a trajectory that culminated in the Turks' recapture of Smyrna and their atrocious massacre of the Christian population of that city. A month later an armistice was concluded, and the following year saw the harrowing exchange of populations between the two implacably hostile states.

The manuscript for this draft offers the following significant variants:

LINE 8   and the attitude of the Greeks is rather dubious

OR   Similarly, what's said about the feelings of the
        Greeks is rather dubious, it seems to me

LINE 23   The Macedonian is a warlike race, wise poet

LINE 25   and because of his great girth and slothfulness

The Dynasty pg. 15

Dated November 1923 on the covering sheet (the first of a total of four), which also gives the title. The front of sheet 2 contains the text of the poem, while the back gives a page reference to a passage from Bouché-Leclercq's *Histoire des Séleucides* about Cleopatra III "the Scarlet." The third sheet lists the three titles Cavafy considered for this poem, and also contains the variant for line 7. On sheet 4 the poet made the following note: "In connection with the degrading *sobriquets* of the Ptolemies something has been written in a number of 'Pharos' early 1925; or late 1926."

This poem stands as perhaps Cavafy's most trenchant editorial comment on the moral and political disintegration of the Hellenistic Greek monarchies during the second century B.C., when Rome was assuming world hegemony—a disintegration all too apparent in the contemptuous nicknames that the Alexandrians lavished on their corrupt rulers. For PTOLEMY VIII "PHYSKON" ("POTBELLY"), see above on "Ptolemy the Benefactor (or Malefactor)." Physkon had several children by his second wife, his niece and stepdaughter Cleopatra III, a scheming woman who was nicknamed Kokkê, "THE SCARLET" (the term was also vulgar slang for the female genitalia). These children included two daughters also named Cleopatra, as well as two warring brothers, Ptolemy IX Soter II (c. 141–81), rather mysteriously nicknamed Lathyrus, "CHICKPEA," and Ptolemy X Alexander I (c. 180–88), nicknamed Epeisaktos, "INTERLOPER," because of his mother's schemes to put him on the throne. (Despite this favoritism, he is said to have had a hand in her death.) Each, at various points, ruled Cyprus after having been driven from Egypt by his brother, only to return later on.

As this poem and its predecessor in this series make clear, Cavafy is well and wryly aware of the striking parallels between two generations of Ptolemies: Ptolemy VI and his brother, Ptolemy VIII; and the latter Ptolemy's sons, Ptolemy IX and Ptolemy X. Like their father, both Ptolemy IX and Ptolemy X were co-rulers at various points with powerful mothers and sisters; each brother in both generations was driven from Egypt and briefly ruled a nearby Mediterranean principality (Cyrene in the earlier generation, Cyprus in the later); and in each generation, one of the brothers married the daughter of the other—in each case, a woman named Cleopatra.

There are significant variants for the following lines:

LINE 6   chaffers and quick wits, gave them excellent

LINE 5–7   The Alexandrian
               people, quick-witted, really gave them
               the right names: more suitable for them are

The two other titles that the poet had contemplated were "Potbelly's Sons" and "House of Potbelly."

From the Unpublished History   pg. 16

November 1923. The dossier consists of only two sheets, the first noting the title and the date and the second containing the text of the poem on the front, written, as Lavagnini observes, quickly and with almost no corrections, apart from a pair of short false starts for the first line, after which the verses flow freely and without interruption. On the back of sheet 2 the poet noted a reference to his source material.

The swift and assured composition of this short poem derives, Lavagnini observes, from the poet's recent reading of his source material, an anecdote about the Byzantine emperor JUSTINIAN (483–565), often referred to as "the last Roman emperor." Born near what is now Skopje in present-day Macedonia, he was the nephew of Justin I, the talented if nearly illiterate commoner who went on to become a great general and then emperor (for whom see the note on "If Indeed He Died," in *Collected Poems*). Justinian is best known for the magisterial revision of the Roman legal code that was undertaken at his behest; for the remarkable reassertion of imperial power in the West—the last such before what had been the Western Empire was lost forever to the Germanic tribes—under the great general Belisarius; and of course for his marriage to the dynamic, lowborn, and highly colorful empress Theodora, a former courtesan. Among the noteworthy events of his reign was the Byzantine state's takeover of Plato's Academy in Athens, which for a millennium had been the symbolic source of pagan Hellenic culture and the training ground of its great intellectual emissaries—a final and symbolically resonant absorption of the pagan Greek past into the Christian Greek present.

Much of what we know of Justinian's reign derives primarily from the works of the historian Procopius, a contemporary of Justinian's who served on the staff of Belisarius. For many years these works were thought to consist of *On the Wars,* comprising a total of eight volumes dedicated to the emperor's military exploits through the year 552—a work Procopius was eminently well suited to write, given his intimacy with Belisarius's numerous campaigns—and "On Buildings," a panegyric to the emperor's building programs. Only after the author's death (probably in the 560s) did another, remarkably different account of Justinian's reign come to light: the so-called *Secret History* (the Greek title, which Cavafy uses in his poem, is simply *Anekdota,* better rendered as the *Unpublished* [i.e., *History* or *Writings*]). Here, the historian allows himself to indulge in vicious criticism of the emperor and his wife impossible to express in his official history. No little of the vituperation expressed in the Unpublished History, which is full of scandalous and, often, pornographic gossip about Justinian and Theodora, derived from the wellborn Procopius's resentment—shared by many of his class—of Justinian's use of talented commoners, or "new men," in the energetic administration of the newly revivified empire; although it is also true that dissatisfaction with the emperor grew over the years of his long reign, which included a devastating plague that decimated the empire throughout the east.

The source for the present poem is one we can pinpoint with some accuracy, thanks to Cavafy's note on the back of the second sheet: page 424 of the second volume of J. B. Bury's *A History of the Later Roman Empire from the Death of Theodosius I to the Death of Justinian* (395–565), published in London in 1923. That the draft of this poem is dated so soon after the book's publication indicates how eager the poet was to get his hands on Bury's new work. (We know that he had already read and made notes on the British historian's 1889 *History of the Later Roman Empire from Arcadius to Irene* [395 A.D. to 800 A.D.]) Here is the passage in question (to provide proper context, I begin the citation on the preceding page):

The thesis of the *Secret History* is that in all the acts of his public policy Justinian was actuated by two motives, rapacity and an inhuman delight in evil-doing and destruction. In this policy he was aided by Theodora, and if they appeared in certain matters, such as religion, to pursue different ends, this was merely a plot designed to hoodwink the public. Procopius gravely asserts that he himself and "most of us" had come to the conclusion that the Emperor and Empress were demons in human form, and he did not mean this as a figure of speech. He tells a number of anecdotes to substantiate the idea. Justinian's mother had once said that she conceived of a demon. He had been seen in the palace at night walking about without a head, and a clairvoyant monk had once refused to enter the presence chamber because he saw the chief of the demons sitting on the throne. Before her marriage, Theodora had dreamt that she would cohabit with the prince of the devils.

The passage in Procopius's *Secret History* to which Bury refers (12.14–21) is the following one:

> Wherefore to me, and many others of us, these two seemed not to be human beings, but veritable demons, and what the poets call vampires: who laid their heads together to see how they could most easily and quickly destroy the race and deeds of men; and assuming human bodies, became man-demons, and so convulsed the world. And one could find evidence of this in many things, but especially in the super-human power with which they worked their will.
>
> For when one examines closely, there is a clear difference between what is human and what is supernatural. There have been many enough men, during the whole course of history, who by chance or by nature have inspired great fear, ruining cities or countries or whatever else fell into their power; but to destroy all men and bring calamity on the whole inhabited earth remained for these two to accomplish, whom Fate

aided in their schemes of corrupting all mankind. For by earthquakes, pestilences, and floods of river waters at this time came further ruin, as I shall presently show. Thus not by human, but by some other kind of power they accomplished their dreadful designs.

And they say his mother said to some of her intimates once that not of Sabbatius her husband, nor of any man was Justinian a son. For when she was about to conceive, there visited a demon, invisible but giving evidence of his presence perceptibly where man consorts with woman, after which he vanished utterly as in a dream.

And some of those who have been with Justinian at the palace late at night, men who were pure of spirit, have thought they saw a strange demoniac form taking his place. One man said that the Emperor suddenly rose from his throne and wandered about, and indeed he was never wont to remain sitting for long, and immediately Justinian's head vanished, while the rest of his body seemed to make these same extensive rounds; whereat the beholder stood aghast and fearful, wondering if his eyes were deceiving him. But presently he perceived the vanished head filling out and join-ing the body again as strangely as it had left it. (tr. Richard Atwater, with modifications)

Lavagnini notes that Cavafy must have consulted Procopius directly, in addition to reading Bury: she cites "late" in line 6 of the poem (cf. Pro-copius, "late at night") and the variant for line 7, "went about/the hall-ways of the palace" (cf. Procopius, "make these same extensive rounds"), details absent from Bury's paraphrase.

Given the meticulousness of Cavafy's reading of source material, and his habit of comparing contemporary historians with those original sources, it is worth citing the assessment (p. 424) of Procopius's relia-bility as a source with which Bury follows his paraphrase of the ancient historian's gossipy account:

[I]t may be asked whether the book deserves any serious con-sideration as an historical document, except so far as it illustrates the intense dissatisfaction prevailing in some circles against the government.

Bury then goes on to say that the attitude toward the government shown in *On the Wars* is "not inconsistent" with that shown in the *Secret History,* and concludes that "the *Secret History* therefore is a document of which the historian is entitled to avail himself, but he must remember that here the author has probably used, to a greater extent than elsewhere, material derived from gossip which he could not verify himself."

The Rescue of Julian *pg. 17*

December 1923. The dossier consists of five sheets, the first giving the title and date.

Following the death of CONSTANTINE in 337, his three sons, Constantine II, Constantius, and Constans divided the empire among them, per their father's will: Constantius, however, is said to have had a hand in the massacre of nearly all of his late father's male relations. Among the murdered men was JULIUS CONSTANTIUS, the late emperor's half brother, whose two small children, Gallus (then aged twelve) and JULIAN (the future emperor, then aged six), were the only two survivors of the coup. In the account of Gregory of Nazianzus, a favorite Cavafian source, Julian was "saved together with his brother" by Christian priests, who spirited the boys to a church, where they took refuge near an altar—an "unlikely, incredible rescue." That Cavafy originally derived his inspiration from Gregory's account is clear not merely from the fact that his poem reproduces details from it (such as Nazianzus's word *paradoxon,* "incredible," to describe the rescue in the second stanza), but because the early forms of the poem refer to both princes being rescued. And indeed the two original titles were "The Rescue of Gallus and Julian" and "The Rescue of the Small Children of Julius Constantius." At a certain point, however, Cavafy evidently consulted another favorite source, the three-volume biography of Julian by the French historian Paul Allard, in which only Julian is mentioned as the object of the priests' rescue; a note left by the poet in the dossier for this poem states that "Allard speaks only about Julian." The doubt that Allard's version placed in the poet's mind evidently caused the ever-scrupulous Cavafy to revise the poem in progress, eliminating references to the older brother and changing the title.

Whatever their origins in a wholly typical desire for strict historical accuracy, the revisions had the salutary effect of focusing the poem on Julian alone—a narrowing that adds an even sharper point to the final verse, which highlights Julian's own dismissive (and, in view of the events recalled here, appallingly ungrateful) attitude toward his early life as a Christian. The Apostate began his fourth oration, on the sun god Helios, with a recollection of his early days, when he was still a professed Christian (and yet, he claims, even then deeply attracted to the sun god). He interrupts this reverie with the following exclamation:

> But why do I mention these things, having more important things to talk about, if I should talk about how I used to think about the gods in those days? Let there be no memory of that darkness [i.e., his early days as a Christian].

That oblivion conveniently elides the heroic bravery of the Christian priests to whom he owed his life. Here as elsewhere, the quality in Julian that Cavafy particularly detests is his hypocrisy.

Gibbon, like Cavafy, understood that both the apostate emperor's character and his bizarre ideology were formed during the traumas of a violent childhood, although he shows himself somewhat more sympathetic to Julian than our poet is:

> The cause of his strange and fatal apostasy may be derived from the early period of his life, when he was left an orphan in the hands of the murderers of his family. The names of Christ and of Constantius, the ideas of slavery and of religion, were soon associated in a youthful imagination, which was susceptible of the most lively impressions.

The Photograph *pg. 18*

August 1924. The poem exists in a single draft written on the second of the two sheets that constitute this dossier, the first giving title and date.

Cavafy's interest in photographs and photography is already evident in several of the Unpublished Poems: "That's How" (*1913*); "The Bandaged Shoulder" (*1919*), and "From the Drawer" (*1923*). Moreover, the poet's chronological listing of poems from 1891 to 1925 refers to a work, apparently no longer extant, called "The Photograph," dated 1904. What relation that poem and the present draft have to each other is uncertain—this unfinished draft of 1924 could indeed be an attempt at revision and recasting of the earlier poem—but at any rate we can see that the poet's interest in photography dates at least to the beginning of the century, and was a particular preoccupation in the 1920s.

That interest should not surprise us, given that Cavafy's perception of photography as a medium for the preservation of beauty, long after the material reality of the beauty in question has faded to dust, is remarkably similar to his conception of the role of memory and poetry. In "That's How," the photograph allows the narrator to

> remain
> the face of dreams, a figure
> fashioned for and dedicated to Greek pleasure

And in "From the Drawer," the photograph that the narrator keeps in a special drawer, never to be framed or displayed, is clearly a memento of a forbidden love which, were it to be seen, might trigger embarrassing questions.

There are two noteworthy variants:

LINE 1   Looking at the photograph of a youth fashioned in Beauty

LINES 2–3   (lost forever more: —the photograph had a date of thirty years before

The dates referred to in the drafts of this poem—which is to say, the early to mid-1890s—place the taking of the photograph in the period of the poet's intellectual and artistic ferment, one in which he also seems to have struggled to come to terms with his homosexuality. For a detailed discussion of Cavafy's artistic transformation during the 1890s, see the Introduction to *Collected Poems,* pp. xxvi–xli.

The Seven Holy Children   *pg. 19*

January 1925. The dossier consists of three sheets, the first bearing the title and the date. One side of the second sheet contains lines 1–13 of the last version, with minor corrections. The reverse of the same sheet contains, again with minor corrections, lines 15–22, along with a much-corrected draft of parts of the last stanza. The last form of the remainder of that stanza, together with further crossings-out and corrections, appear on the third sheet.

The remarkable, fairy tale–like legend of the Seven Sleepers (or "SEVEN HOLY CHILDREN"), well known to Greeks, is retailed in the third volume of the three-volume *synaxarion,* or biographical calendar of saints' feast days, that Cavafy is known to have owned and which shows signs of attentive reading—and from which he meticulously quotes here, thereby lending his poem a certain ecclesiastical color. The seven children in question were said to have been brothers living in EPHESUS, the great city on the coast of Asia Minor; in order to flee the vicious persecutions of Christians that were set in motion by the emperor Decius (201–251) in 250, they took refuge in a cave near the city. (Cavafy's *synaxarion* sets this particular event in the year 252, which is to say, after Decius had died.) After the cave was walled up by the persecutors, the children entrusted their souls to God, and then fell asleep. They woke on what they thought was the next morning but, according to Cavafy's source, turned out to be the thirty-eighth year of the reign of Theodosius II (401–450; acceded 408)—i.e., the year 446. (Their sleep, therefore, indeed lasted for the "two centuries" Cavafy refers to in his poem, and not the 372 years to which his *synaxarion* rather mysteriously refers.) Not knowing that the empire had by this time been Christianized, one of their number, IAMBLICHUS, nervously went out to the city to buy bread. As he traveled through an uncannily altered Ephesus—there was, he observed, a cross decorating the city gate—he thought that the people seemed different; among other things, the baker looked askance at the outdated coinage with which he tried to pay for his bread. (In one version of the story, resentful citizens assume that the seven boys have come across a cache of old Decian coinage.) Soon enough the miraculous truth of what had happened became clear, and in order to marvel at the wonderful children even the emperor, the pious and scholarly THEODOSIUS, came from Constantinople. The conclusion of the story, in which the exhausted boys soon fell asleep again forever, was seen as a prefiguration of the Resurrection.

The legend, which seems to have originated in a Syriac version (in which there were eight children), goes back at least as far as the late 500s, when it was translated into Latin by Gregory of Tours (ca. 540 to 593–94), that aristocratic bishop and avid chronicler of history and miracles. The cave where the Seven hid and the cemetery in Ephesus where they were buried were the object of pilgrimages by the devout, and indeed the earliest evidence we have for the veneration of these saints is a visit to their tomb by a pilgrim in the 530s. Gibbon, who gives a splendid retelling of the legend in chapter 33 of the *Decline and Fall,* and who was particularly impressed by its cross-cultural appeal (he notes that it appears in the Koran), saw it as a parable about men's relation to history: "We imperceptibly advance from youth to age, without observing the gradual, but incessant, change in human affairs." Cavafy is sure to have been acquainted with Gibbon's version and analysis as well as with the reference in the *synaxarion.*

Cavafy's interest in early Christian themes is evident in his earliest work: under one of his thematic headings, "The Beginnings of Christianity," were grouped six poems, of which only two survived the poet's Philosophical Scrutiny of 1903–1904: "Julian at Eleusis" (written in 1896, then given the title "Julian at the Mysteries") and "The Cross," written in 1892 and revised in 1917, which was very likely the original version of "A Great Procession of Priests and Laymen," published in its final form in 1926. We know the titles of the others from his chronological indices: "The Return [of] C[ono]n" (1892); "The Temptation of the Syrian Monk Thaddeus" (1892, rewritten in 1902 as "The Temptation of the Syrian Ascetic Thaddeus"); "Porphyry" (1892); and "Saint Stephanus" (1898). This besetting interest in early Christianity, although superseded in time by other enthusiasms, resurfaced by the late 1910s, as is evident in the Unpublished Poem "Simeon" (*1917:* see the note in *Collected Poems* on the lengthy marginal comment, dating to the mid-1890s, that Cavafy made in his copy of Gibbon, expressing admiration for Simeon Stylites).

As Lavagnini notes, the poet's particular interest in the Seven Sleepers of Ephesus at this time is evident in a note that he made on seeing a reference to the legend in a source that was distinctly unreligious: the eighth pastiche in Proust's *Pastiches et mélanges,* which were first collected in book form in 1919. In the context of a renewed attention to this legend at this point in the poet's career, it is perhaps not too much to wonder whether a certain correction that he consistently made in revising the present poem is significant: in the last three stanzas, the word *paides,* "children," in the phrase "Seven Holy Children," which appears in the last version, has replaced the original reading *neoi,* "young men." It is interesting to think that Cavafy began by having in his mind's eye seven *young men* who fell into the miraculous languor to which the legend refers: the experiences of what we might call attractively declining young men during the early Christian era seem to be very much present in his mind already in the mid-1910s, when he composed most of the poems that take the form of funerary inscriptions; and certainly persists through the mid- to late 1920s, as for instance in "Cleitus's Illness" (1926) and "Myres: Alexandria in 340 A.D." (1929).

Among the Groves of the Promenades *pg. 21*

The dossier containing the four sheets of paper associated with this poem bears no date; the first sheet, on which the poet normally records the title and date, contains only the title. Lavagnini points out, however, that the paper on which the one complete draft is written is the same as that on which "The Seven Holy Children," dated January 1925, was written; further evidence for a date of 1925 is the fact that Cavafy wrote and published another poem about Apollonius in that year, "Apollonius of Tyana in Rhodes." Alternatively, a date of 1920 is also attractive: in that year Cavafy was working on another draft about a "telepathic" vision of the death of a tyrant ("Athanasius") and it was also the year in which he revised and published "If Indeed He Died," also about Apollonius and his supernatural powers.

The dossier notes an alternate title: "Apollonius of Tyana Seeing from Ephesus What Was Transpiring in Rome."

The sage and magician APOLLONIUS OF TYANA (a town in the Roman province of Cappadocia, in central Asia Minor) was a figure of enduring fascination for Cavafy, who was clearly intimately familiar with the sprawling, rather baroque *Life of Apollonius of Tyana* by the third-century littérateur Flavius Philostratus (ca. 170–240 A.D.), a distinguished man of letters of Greek origin who was a favorite of Julia Domna, wife of the emperor Septimius Severus. An itinerant Neopythagorean philosopher who lived through much of the first century A.D., Apollonius is reported to have traveled widely, as far as Ethiopia and India; he was renowned, after his death, both for his defiance of Roman despots (the climax of the first half of the *Life* is a confrontation with Nero; the climax of the second half, a confrontation with Domitian) and for his magical powers, which included the ability not only to heal the sick and raise the dead, but to see into the near future. (Philostratus's *Life*, composed as Christianity was rising to its ultimate power in Roman society, later became a useful text for those seeking to present the philosophical and miracle-working Oriental Greek as a pagan rival to Christ.) He allegedly predicted, for instance, a plague that struck the city of Ephesus in Asia Minor, and it was this prediction that was later held against him, when he was accused, by an Egyptian enemy, of various crimes and impieties, among them sorcery. Apollonius was subsequently tried before the notoriously cruel emperor, Domitian (Titus Flavius Domitianus, 51–96 A.D.). In the *Life*, the trial scene—a grand occasion for displays of rhetorical dazzle—takes up nearly all of the final book. (For detailed analysis of the importance of Apollonius in Cavafy's work, see the Note in *Collected Poems*, pp. 357–60.)

The title of the present poem, which is a verbatim quotation from the *Life*, is an allusion to another famous "telepathic" incident, which takes place after Apollonius has returned to Ephesus following his trial: the sage's miraculous vision, while he was strolling in a grove of trees adorning a promenade in Ephesus, of the bloody assassination of Domitian in Rome. (Having been stabbed by an attendant called Stephanus, the emperor fought back using a golden goblet as a weapon, but eventually succumbed when more conspirators joined in.) The incident is described in detail in chapter 26 of the final book of the *Life*, and elements in Cavafy's poetic account of it again suggest how closely he followed his sources:

All of this [the assassination] happened in Rome, but Apollonius observed it in Ephesus. He was holding a discussion among the groves of the promenades about noon, the very time when the events in the palace took place. First he dropped his voice, as if afraid, and then began to express himself with less than his usual power, as people do who observe something different in the middle of a speech, and then fell silent, as people do when breaking their speech off. He stared hard at the ground, stepped three or four paces forward, and shouted, "Strike the tyrant! Strike!" not as if he was drawing some reflection of reality from a mirror, but seeing the actual thing and seeming to take part in the action.

All the Ephesians were present at the lecture, and were astounded until Apollonius, after waiting as people do to watch the outcome of a close contest, said, "Have no fear, gentlemen, since the tyrant was slaughtered today. Why do I say today? Just now, I swear by Athena, just now, about the moment when I fell silent in my talk." (tr. C. P. Jones, with some emendations)

The three Published Poems about Apollonius are "But Wise Men Apprehend What Is Imminent" (*1896*; *1899*; *1915*), "If Indeed He Died" (*1897*; *1910*; *1920*), and "Apollonius of Tyana in Rhodes" (*?*; *1925*).

The first lines of this poem, with their evocation of the ruinous effect that Domitian had on the provinces of the empire, stands in contrast to an observation that Cavafy made in one of the letters he wrote to Alexander Sengopoulos between 1918 and 1919, apropos of his recent reading of Suetonius:

I've been reading lately—in translation—Suetonius. He's not of great value. His famous work is the biographies of the first twelve emperors of Rome. I've been reading that. It had the advantage of being anecdotal and one learns a lot or guesses it from what he says, about the social life of the time. One thing the student of imperial Rome should have in view is that the miserable situation in the capital doesn't at all imply the same situation in the state in general. For one thing, the slowness and difficulty of communications, and for another the good and orderly organization of the different parts of the Roman state, often brought it about that a bad emperor, who did harm in Rome, did none in the provinces. (Quoted in Robert Liddell, *Cavafy: A Biography* [Duckworth, 1974], p. 172)

Variants:

LINE 5   in the groves where the statues were, he seemed

LINE 10   in that moment
when the preeminent magus was distracted,
in that very moment his soul had seen

LINE 13   And he himself had beaten
Stephanus afterward: with a golden chalice
he'd beaten him horribly; and finally the crowds

OR   And he himself, after, had thrown
Stephanus down: with a golden chalice

The Patriarch   *pg. 22*

February 1925. The dossier contains a total of seven sheets, of which the first records the title—which the poet notes is only "provisional"—and the date of original composition. Sheet 2 contains the earliest draft of the poem, which is heavily reworked in places; on sheet 3 only the phrase "that worthy man" appears; sheet 4 contains, along with some variants to lines on sheet 2, the passage from the Byzantine historical work that is cited verbatim in the long variant which appears on sheet 5. Lavagnini notes that fully two years elapsed between the first version of this draft and subsequent rewriting: the stationery of sheet 5 bears a colophon with the date 1927. Sheets 6 and 7 contain variants to the last six lines of the text on sheet 2.

The text reproduced here is the last form of the draft appearing on sheet 2; variants are noted below.

This poem, along with "On Epiphany," both dating to 1925, makes it clear that during the mid-1920s Cavafy was very much preoccupied with the Byzantine emperor JOHN VI CANTACUZENUS (ca. 1295–June 15, 1383; reigned 1347–1354); these two Unfinished Poems take their place beside the Published Poems "John Cantacuzenus Triumphs" (1924) and "Of Colored Glass" (1925) to form a mini cycle within Cavafy's work, a sequence of significant poems devoted to a figure—ambitious, patriotic, devout, generous in victory and noble in defeat—for whom the poet evidently felt no little emotion, and considerable admiration. A long note on Cantacuzenus and his significance in Cavafy's work can be found in Collected Poems, pp. 363–8.

Cantacuzenus was the loyal friend, closest adviser, and general of Emperor Andronicus III Palaeologus. When Andronicus died in 1341, he left a son (later John V), aged nine; his will directed that Cantacuzenus, who held the important title of Great Domestic, be regent for the minor sovereign. However, the regency was almost immediately challenged by a powerful faction at court led by the tremendously ambitious admiral Apocaucus and the scheming PATRIARCH of Constantinople, John XIV Calecas (whom Cantacuzenus—as he reminded the patriarch in a bitter letter cited by the Byzantine historian Nicephorus Gregoras, a contemporary of Cantacuzenus and a source Cavafy consulted for this poem—had helped to secure the patriarchate in 1334). These men together persuaded the widowed empress, Anna of Savoy, that her dead husband's friend was planning to usurp the throne, and after Anna claimed control of the boy herself, the three began a campaign of vicious harassment against Cantacuzenus and his party that ultimately resulted in the Civil War of 1341–1347. This interlude proved to be one of the most disastrous and demoralizing in the history of the empire: during the six years before Cantacuzenus returned in triumph and took the throne for himself, Anna and her party denuded the empire's treasuries. As a result, Cantacuzenus and his queen were forced to wear regalia made of paste during their coronation at the conclusion of the Civil War: an episode that furnished the material for "Of Colored Glass."

Although Cavafy, as we know from his reading notes to Gibbon, was often impatient with the latter's disdainful view of Byzantium, the two men are united in their admiration for Cantacuzenus, who even as he was forced into open rebellion by the outrages committed against himself, his friends, and his family by Anna and her party, clung to the forms of law and resisted the temptation of revenge once he had achieved victory. In February 1347, he stormed his way into the city and, with remarkable but characteristic even-handedness, forced the empress to accept quite reasonable terms, which stipulated that he be crowned emperor, with the fifteen-year-old John Palaeologus as co-emperor. ("John Cantacuzenus Triumphs" takes the form of a monologue by a disappointed supporter of Anna and the patriarch. To such former enemies, Cantacuzenus showed admirable generosity.) But relations between the two co-emperors soon deteriorated, and another civil war broke out. This time, Cantacuzenus was defeated by John V and in 1354 was forced to abdicate. He thereafter became a monk, calling himself Joasaph, and during his monastic retirement devoted himself to matters theological and to writing his memoirs in four books, the *Historiai* or "Histories" (to which "On Epiphany," below, refers).

The quality of having persisted in his political life with no little dignity against tremendous odds and of then having retreated from the world stage with an equal dignity clearly captivated Cavafy's imagination. We might compare the poet's apparent approval for the quiet abdication of Demetrius Poliorcetes in "King Demetrius," and, by contrast, his disdain for the self-serving quality of the histories written by the scheming Anna Comnena in her forced retirement ("Anna Comnena").

The present poem, like "On Epiphany," is pervaded by lingering bitterness about the perfidy of Anna and her two cohorts. It is in fact inhabited by four characters named John, two present in the poem and two only alluded to—one of them with characteristically delicate Cavafian subtlety. An appreciation of its bitter ironies rests on a proper understanding of the relationship among the four.

The noble character of John Cantacuzenus, the first John, is plain: the poet's emotional regard for him is signaled by, among other things, the use of the charged phrase "the worthy man whom our race then possessed" in line 5, the possessive pronoun here as elsewhere marking a nostalgic pride in Byzantium (see the note on "After the Swim," pp. 53–6), as the Cavafy scholar Diana Haas has noted. The contrast with the second John, the scheming John Calecas, could not, of course, be greater. The particular object of the narrator's scorn is the hypocrit-ical claim by the ambitious patriarch that Cantacuzenus was seeking to seize the throne from the rightful heir, Andronicus's underage son—the poem's third John. In making this outrageous claim, Calecas had disin-genuously alluded to events of almost exactly one hundred years earlier involving yet another underage heir named John, the fourth John of this poem. In 1258, the seven-year-old JOHN LASCARIS succeeded to the throne of his father, Emperor Theodore II Lascaris, but he was soon deposed by the powerful aristocrat Michael Palaeologus with the per-haps reluctant complicity of the boy's guardian, the patriarch ARSENIUS (the latter referred to in some variant lines here). After a few years as co-emperor with John, Michael seized the throne for himself, hav-ing ordered his men to blind the boy (thereby disqualifying him from the throne). He then crowned himself emperor as Michael VIII, thus establishing the Palaeologue dynasty—the dynasty to which John Can-tacuzenus's young charge, the subject of the intrigues described in the present poem, belonged. The final irony that hangs over this draft owes much to an awareness that this dynasty owed its origins to a usurpation that the noble Cantacuzenus, rather than Calecas (as he himself hypo-critically claims), is eager not to see repeated.

Sheet 4 of the dossier for this poem contains the poet's transcription of Calecas's hypocritical charge against Cantacuzenus, which he found in Nicephorus Gregoras's history:

> Must the affairs of the Byzantines now be afflicted by up-heavals of the sort that occurred in former times, through the childishness and carelessness of the patriarch at the time, Arsenius? I will therefore throw my lot in with the empress; and I myself shall protect the safety of the young king.

Sheet 5 offers a long variant that quotes the patriarch Calecas's disin-genuous words about that earlier, hapless patriarch, adding outraged interjections on the part of the narrator:

> . . . but did his utmost
> to prevent the upheavals "of the sort that

occurred in former times through the childishness
and carelessness of the patriarch at the time
Arsenius. I" (*I* ! His utmost)
"will therefore throw my lot in with
the empress" (we've come far!);
"And I myself shall protect the young
king's safety."

Gibbon, in an account of the coup d'état of Anna of Savoy, Apocaucus, and Calecas with which Cavafy was familiar, dryly notes that "the founder of the Palaeologi had instructed his posterity to dread the example of a perfidious guardian"—this being the pretext used by Anna and her party to wrest power from Cantacuzenus, although the perfidy was, of course, theirs.

There is a final and particularly bitter layer of irony that hangs over all the Cantacuzenus poems, of which Cavafy, like any student of Late Byzantine history, would have been well aware, and which is impossible not to bear in mind given the date of composition of these poems in the mid-1920s—which is to say, after the disastrous conclusion of the Greco-Turkish War in 1922–1923 (see note on "Ptolemy the Benefactor [or Malefactor]," pp. 58–63). For in order to gain the upper hand against Apocaucus's forces, Cantacuzenus successfully concluded an alliance with the Ottoman emir Orhan (cemented by a marriage between his daughter, Theodora Cantacuzene, and the Muslim leader); but the use of many thousands of Turkish troops, who successfully fought for John in his war against Anna and Apocaucus in the early 1340s and then again, a decade later, helped John in his campaign in the Balkans, was the step that led to the establishment of a permanent Turkish presence in the European continent, and eventually resulted in the Ottoman conquest of the Balkans. Hence John, so warmly described in the present poem as "the glory of our [Byzantine] race," may be seen as being ultimately responsible for the defeat of that race. This is the conclusion to which Gibbon bitterly came:

> To acquire the friendship of their emirs, the two factions
> vied with each other in baseness and profusion: the dexterity

of [John] Cantacuzene obtained the preference: but the succor and victory were dearly purchased by the marriage of his daughter with an infidel, the captivity of many thousand Christians, and the passage of the Ottomans into Europe, the last and fatal stroke in the fall of the Roman empire.

That fall was the cultural, ideological, and historical disaster which the "Megali Idea" was meant to correct: a great idea that, as we know—and as Cavafy knew, when he was working on these poems—ended in dreadful disaster after the Greek defeat in the Greco-Turkish War of 1919–1922.

On Epiphany *pg. 23*

December 1925. The covering sheet for this poem bears the title and the date; the word "May" has been written above the word "Dec[ember]." The dossier consists of four sheets altogether, of which the covering sheet is the first. Sheet 2 contains the text of the first two stanzas; and sheets 3 and 4 contain variant versions of the final stanza.

The crisis that led to the Civil War of 1341–1347 between John Cantacuzenus and the faction of Anna of Savoy, Apocaucus, and the Patriarch Calecas (see above on "The Patriarch") was specially marked by the gross ill-treatment of John's family by his enemies, who had control of the boy emperor. A carefully coordinated (and funded) campaign of insults, rumors, and allegations of treachery against John culminated at Christmastide 1341, after John had been declared a public enemy and his aged mother, the great noblewoman Theodora Palaeologina Cantacuzene, imprisoned in a cell in the royal palace. The ill-treatment of his mother was particularly painful to John, an only child who had been brought up by the widowed Theodora, who, according to his *Histories,* was a woman well known for her high intelligence, ability, and "more than feminine strength of mind." As the account of Nicephorus Gregoras makes clear, the party of Anne of Savoy took advantage of the Christmas Eve vigil to whip up popular resentment against the Cantacuzeni, an outpouring that the demoralized and increasingly ill old woman was forced to listen to from her prison cell, where she was

shamefully ill-treated by the guards set by Apocaucus. This bit of dema-
goguery was to be repeated twelve days later, on Epiphany (January 6,
1342), the day on which Theodora finally died.

The final stanza of this poem invites the reader to compare two
accounts of Theodora's wretched last days. The first is that of Gregoras,
a source to whom Cavafy often turns. An exact contemporary of Can-
tacuzenus (he was born around 1292, and died in 1360), Gregoras was
a distinguished humanist of a type much in evidence in the later Byzan-
tine empire. He rose to prominence under the emperor Andronicus II
Palaeologus, who appointed him Keeper of the Archives when he was
still quite young; not the least of his attainments was a series of propos-
als for the reform of the calendar, which were rejected at the time but
were nearly identical to those ultimately adopted by Pope Gregory two
centuries later. Among his many writings may be counted theological
texts, orations, a treatise about the wanderings of Odysseus, and astro-
nomical and calendrical treatises; his most significant work, however,
was a thirty-seven-volume *Roman History* ("Roman" here referring to
what we call "Byzantine"), which covered in exhaustive detail the years
from 1204 to 1359. It is on this work that Cavafy relies for his account
of the reign of John Cantacuzenus in this poem and the others of the
Cantacuzenus cycle.

And yet as Cavafy was aware, Gregoras's style can be overwrought
and bombastic, and the tension between these qualities—which are
more than evident in the passage describing the events treated in the
present poem—and those of Cantacuzenus's own account of the same
events, in his *Histories*, is the fulcrum of this poem.

After describing the frenzied scene outside the palace on Christmas
Eve—with the seething and clotted mob, encouraged by Apocaucus's
bribes, both cheering the boy emperor and spewing vile invectives
against Cantacuzenus and his mother—Gregoras paints a poignant if
rather overdone picture of the aged lady's private agonies:

> Cantacuzenus's mother heard all these things herself, inhab-
> iting as she did a cell within the royal palace, whither the
> mass of the populace was coursing together in veritable
> rivers, gathering force. And verily her heart was greatly

afflicted, and from her very depths she gave forth lamentations, like turbid and misty clouds of smoke, which made plain to those nearby her soul's great bitterness. Riven in her soul by the unendurable noise of the insults, and considering by whom all this was being staged, they who only yesterday and two days before were as slaves before her, and at the same time casting her memory back to the fortune she had enjoyed since childhood, the flower of youthful happiness that until old age had remained unsullied and freshly blooming, and comparing all of that to the quite opposite and unimaginable issue of Time, she could not bear it; but stricken deep in her heart, she gave her body up to a grave illness which promised that the end of her life was not far off.

When, therefore, the celebration of Epiphany came twelve days later, and the [boy] emperor made his appearance from on high as he had done before, and the people below thundered the same cheers and insults, the Lady Cantacuzene lay dead before her cell, cast aside and utterly forgotten, by now the very image of her former happiness and glory; for she had broken from this life just before the sounding of the trumpets. For her soul, as I think, fearing lest it descend once more into the tempest of those insults, girded itself up and broke forth from her body. And how it was that God contrived that these things should happen, I shall discuss more broadly as I proceed, endeavoring to do so as much as it is possible for me.

To this florid and overwrought account, the narrative of Cantacuzenus—who, obviously, had good reason to feel deeply about the events he was recounting—stands, in its narrative control and emotional restraint, almost as a reproach. In the third book of his four-book *Histories,* the former emperor also describes at great length the way in which the mob had been incited to insult him and his family: he does so in considerable detail but with a dispassion all the more admirable given that he and his loved ones were the victims of the abuses in question. (We

know that his model, as a historian, was Thucydides, and his account of
this turbulent moment in his own reign, although self-serving to be sure
in many places, reveals a nicely dry Thucydidean turn of phrase now and
then: of the abuses heaped on him and his family he remarks that the
mob "offered this to the young king as if it were a sweet gift.") Later on
in the narrative of his turbulent accession, Cantacuzenus, again with an
impressive stylistic and emotional restraint, describes his mother's final
sufferings (always referring to himself in the third person):

> And the mother of king Cantacuzenus, whom they had first
> thrown in prison, they intentionally maltreated, nor did they
> fail to display to her any kind of meanness. For they set as
> guards for her men both shameless and of savage mind, and
> ordered them to show her every sort of cruelty and to treat
> her as outrageously and contemptuously as possible. Their
> provision of the necessities of nourishment, which earlier
> had been insufficient enough, grew ever more niggardly. And
> if they were to provide her with some porridge, whence
> they might be thought to be charitable, knowing in what lux-
> ury and elegance she had been raised, and that she would
> never touch anything that had been fouled, they would thrust
> their dirty hands in it, making as if to test the porridge to see
> if it concealed letters that had been sent by her son, although
> they themselves had cooked what was being offered her.
> Which seeing, she preferred to die of hunger than to taste of
> such filth. Nor, in the bitter and freezing winter, was she
> afforded the comfort of a fire or of any other necessity,
> although the empress [Anna of Savoy] had ordered that she
> not be deprived of any bodily comfort. Every day the guards
> did not fail to insult her son outrageously in her presence
> and—as if they had just had the news from a messenger—
> they would relate to her sometimes that her son had been
> captured and, suffering shamefully, had been clapped in
> irons; or, at other times, that a battle had taken place in
> which he had been killed and that his head was being borne
> thither, which they promised her they would bring to her, as

a consolation. And they told her other, more savage and by far more inhumane things as well, as a result of which, with her heart boiling over and as if melting, she succumbed to extreme fever. The women about her, greatly imploring those savage keepers in the hopes that they might prevail upon them to send for a doctor and to show her some little consideration, were unable to incite to pity the inner marrow of hard-hearted men who were accustomed daily to feast on the marrow of other human beings. But they denied her all care, slaughtering her as surely as if they had done it with their own hands. Now the empress, having heard from someone that the emperor's mother was ailing and that no order had been given, neither by the magistrates nor by the master of the world and his gentle and humanitarian student, to fetch her a doctor, bitterly reproached them their savagery and hard-heartedness; and she ordered her doctor, who was wont to attend her own illnesses, to go to her and to accord her whatever care was called for. But the patriarch and the rest of that fellowship of goodly men took the doctor aside and forced him to swear that when he had gone in to see her he would do nothing about the illness.

The considerable power of this passage (which cannot have been easy to write, even after the passage of many years) owes much to shrewd use of detail—the porridge story conveys the humiliations of Theodora's captivity with terrific efficiency—and to a bitter but always understated irony (the references to Calecas and his band as "the master of the world and his gentle and humanitarian student," "the patriarch and the rest of that fellowship of goodly men").

Why does the poet invite us to contrast the high-flown and self-serving sentimentality of Gregoras's account with the contained power of Cantacuzenus's narrative? A suggestive clue lies in a variant reading for the final stanza, which reads as follows:

The death of Cantacuzene, so piteous,
I found in the History of Nicephorus Gregoras.

It's written somewhat differently (but not less painfully)
By the historian John Cantacuzenus.

To refer to the former emperor as a "historian," *istorikos,* is a striking ges-
ture—particularly for this poet, for whom the word has a very special
resonance. As we know, Cavafy insisted on referring to himself as a "poet-
historian," and both his poetic corpus and working papers, not least the
dossiers for these Unfinished Poems, everywhere betray a scholarly
meticulousness and deep respect for the methodological and intellectual
standards of the professional historian. (As witness here his reluctance to
publish "Athanasius" until he had located the primary source for the anec-
dote retold in that poem: see above, pp. 48–51.) We might say that the
invitation, in the present poem, to reflect on matters of historiographical
style reminds us that the qualities of understatement and restraint that
Cavafy admired in Cantacuzenus the man are clearly also present in the
qualities of Cantacuzenus's historical text; and it is surely no accident that
these qualities—a meticulously calibrated control and self-effacement, an
eye for the representative and suggestive narrative detail, a stylistic under-
statement effectively contrasted with emotional drama—are qualities
representative of Cavafy's own work. Read against Gregoras's text, we
can see, then, how the phrase "no less sadly" in the last version of the poem
suggests, in a fashion that is allusive but impossible to miss, an artistic
credo: that a great restraint can be a conduit for, rather than an impedi-
ment to, the expression of profound emotion.

Epitaph of a Samian .... *pg. 24*

October 1925. The dossier contains four sheets in all, the first bearing
the title and date. Sheet 2 consists of the text of the 1893 draft of a son-
net, "Epitaph," which Cavafy was here attempting to work into a larger
and more complex frame. The back of sheet 2 contains some rework-
ings of lines from the original sonnet; sheet 3 is a note in English (see
below); and sheet 4 contains, in addition to further revisions to the orig-
inal sonnet, new material meant to comprise a historical frame for the
original epitaph.

The dossier for this vexed attempt at reconfiguring a discarded poem from a much earlier period provides a fascinating insight into Cavafy's creative intelligence. The note in English written on sheet 3 sounds almost plaintive (I quote it in Lavagnini's reconstruction of Cavafy's shorthand):

> A very old poem
> cannot something be
> made of it?

In 1925 the poem in question was indeed more than thirty years old: the sonnet entitled "Epitaph," an Unpublished work dated June 1893 and listed under the heading "Ancient Days," which purports to be the gravestone inscription of a Samian Greek (see *Collected Poems*, p. 499). The various drafts indicate that Cavafy considered a number of alterations to the original sonnet, the most significant of which is a replacement for the second stanza that would have read as follows (a variant worth noting not least because it adds a line that is then quoted in the new "framing" verses the poet wanted to add to the original poem):

> I was utterly worn out, very harshly worked—
> far from my dear Samos, and, terrible to tell
> I spent forty years without
> ever hearing or ever speaking Greek.

The material of greatest interest in this dossier is the seven new lines the poet composed, a supplement that creates a subtle historical frame of a kind familiar from other works. The sonnet itself, in this version, is presented as a poem written by a fictitious poet called Cleonymus, son of Timandrus, described as a favorite poet of the Seleucid monarch ANTIOCHUS IV EPIPHANES (215–163 B.C.). Late Hellenistic evocations of historical incidents or texts of the Classical period constitute a familiar Cavafian device, one that allows the poet to comment with some irony on the discrepancy between the glories of the Greek past and the complex compromises—cultural, historical, and often moral—of the later, decadent present of the "frame." This device seems, if anything, to enjoy special prominence during the mid- to late-1920s, the period of the composition of the present poem: see, for instance, the

Published Poems "Those Who Fought on Behalf of the Achaean League" (1922) and "Temethus, an Antiochene: 400 A.D." (1925), and, among the Unfinished, "Ptolemy the Benefactor (or Malefactor)," also from 1922. As many of the poems—published, unpublished, and unfinished— also demonstrate, the decade of the 1920s saw Cavafy returning again and again, either directly or indirectly, to the period of the collapse of the Seleucid monarchy, a period in which Antiochus IV, a Seleucid whom Cavafy particularly liked to invoke, was a key figure. (See, for instance, "Of Demetrius Soter: 162–150 B.C." [1915; 1919], "Favour of Alexander Balas" [1916; 1921], "Craftsman of Wine-Bowls" [1903; 1912; 1921], "For Antiochus Epiphanes" [1911, 1922], "Temethus, Anti-ochene: 400 A.D." [?; 1925], and the Unfinished Poem "Antiochus the Cyzicene" [1920].)

The framing device, and the preoccupation with the declining Seleucid empire, come together in the present draft, which indicates that although Cavafy had played with various geographical and chronological possibilities, he was intent on integrating the old poem into a new one that had considerably greater complexity and bite. One variant, to the text of the original sonnet, would have placed the Samian's tomb on the banks of the Tigris, a location less fabulously distant from Greek culture than the Ganges. Another variant, on the second line of the framing addition, had the epitaph referring "to times before Alexander [the Great]," an era closer to the fictitious poet's times than is the setting of the last reading ("to a time before the Persian Wars").

Whatever locale and era the Samian belongs to, Cleonymus's emotion—and Cavafy's irony—are clear. The Seleucid poet is full of no little cultural self-satisfaction: writing at a time when the Greek language, under the Hellenistic kingdoms, holds sway throughout much of the former Persian (or "Median") territory, he views with a pitying condescension the anonymous Samian of long ago who was unfortunate enough to live at a time when a Greek traveler in the East would have been lonely for the sound of Greek. (It is worth noting that Hellenic pride in the extent of the spread of the Greek language, particularly to India, is a theme of other later poems: see the Unpublished Poem "Coins" [1920] and the Published Poem "In 200 B.C." [1916?; 1931].) And yet here as in certain other poems whose narrators are full of pride in the magnificent extent and achievements of Hellenistic civilization—

"In 200 B.C." and the Unfinished "Nothing About the Lacedaemonians" and "Agelaus"—the speaker's complacent confidence in the supremacy of his Greek culture is in fact the object of a subtle irony. For as we know, the reign of the philhellenic Antiochus IV saw the end of the Seleucid might of which the court poet in the present poem is so proud; indeed, the great capital of SELEUCIA fell to the Parthians soon after Antiochus's death. (For more on this device, see below on "Nothing About the Lacedaemonians" and "Agelaus," pp. 104–5 and 108–10.)

Cavafy's inspiration for this poem may well have been a passage from the *Life of Apollonius of Tyana* (1.23) that describes the sage's tearful reaction, while traveling near Babylon, on coming across the tombs of Greeks from Eretria who had been captured and deported to Asia by Darius I during the first Persian War. The author of the *Life* goes so far as to quote one of the grave inscriptions, of which Cavafy's sonnet is strongly reminiscent:

> Here now we lie on Ecbatana's plain,
> But once we sailed the deep Aegean's swell.
> Farewell, Eretrian homeland, old in fame,
> And nearby Athens, and the sea, farewell.
>
> (tr. C. P. Jones)

Remorse *pg. 25*

October 1925. The dossier consists of two sheets, the first bearing the title—which the poet notes is "provisional" only—and the date, and the second containing the text of the poem, written swiftly and with few corrections.

In its frankness and the deep yet by no means glib sympathy with which it surveys a complicated and compromised emotional landscape, this poem recalls other, earlier works while surpassing them in its self-assured humaneness—a quality that seems to grow in strength in Cavafy's work as the years pass.

We might compare, for instance, the rather severe ethical vision in poems written at the turn of the century, the years, as we know, when Cavafy was going through his poetic crisis. In "Che fece . . . Il Gran Rifiuto" (*1899; 1901*), for instance, the poet passes a harsh judgment on those who, in moments of moral crisis, choose the path of personal comfort or safety over that of large moral responsibility:

> For certain people there comes a day
> when they are called upon to say the great Yes
> or the great No. It's clear at once who has
> the Yes within him at the ready, which he will say
>
> as he advances in honor, in greater self-belief.
> He who refuses has no second thoughts. Were he asked
> again, he would repeat the No. And nonetheless
> that no—so right—defeats him all his life.

The poet's severity here is all the more striking for being directed at the saintly pope Celestine V, who resigned the papacy at the age of eighty, in 1294—a decision understandable in itself but condemned by Dante (whence the title) because it paved the way, as Celestine knew it must, for the advent of the corrupt and immoral Boniface VIII.

Such unyielding rigor may be seen as the inevitably self-punishing product of a secretive and shamed existence. A yearning for understanding and forgiveness is implied by another poem of the same period, one that focuses less on condemnation than on the speaker's admiration for those who uphold standards of right behavior and decency even in the face of apparently inevitable moral weakness and betrayals such as the ones he disdains in "Che Fece . . . Il Gran Rifiuto." In "Thermopylae" (*1901*; *1903*), Cavafy suggests that another component of the just man's personality is a forgiveness of weaker men. Here the speaker praises those who are

> generous whenever they're rich, and again
> when they're poor, generous in small things,
> and helping out, again, as much as they are able;
> always speaking the truth,
> yet without hatred for those who lie.

Ten years later there is evidence of a still more forgiving vision. In the Unpublished Poem "Hidden" (*1908*), a poem marked by the same plainness of language and remarkable self-exposure that we find in this Unfinished Poem, Cavafy acknowledges quite openly the failure to be open, the necessary concealments and lies which, we know, characterized his early years:

> An obstacle was there and it distorted
> my actions and the way I lived my life.
> An obstacle was there and it stopped me
> on many occasions when I was going to speak.

And yet that poem ends on a note of hope that contains within it the large vision advocated in the opening lines of "Remorse"—the acknowledgment that the individual's problems and failures must be put in a proper perspective:

> But perhaps it's not worth squandering
> so much care and trouble on puzzling me out.
> Afterwards—in some more perfect society—
> someone else who's fashioned like me
> will surely appear and be free to do as he pleases.

In the context of this evolving moral vision, of which the increasing emphasis on forgiveness reflects, perhaps, a growing sense of self-acceptance, "Remorse" might be seen as a culminating ethical and poetic moment.

The Emperor Conon   *pg. 26*

March 1926. The dossier contains three sheets: the first noting the title and the date, the second containing the text of the poem, and a third simply noting the title again.

   The poem refers to the conflict between the Byzantine emperor LEO III (ca. 680–741), who instigated the religious policy known as iconoclasm—the destruction or removal of religious icons, on the grounds that icon worship violated the Second Commandment—and Germanus I, PATRIARCH of Constantinople, who, like many of Leo's subjects, violently opposed the new policy. Leo, born in the Syrian province of Commagene and given the leadership of the eastern armies by Anastasius II, became emperor in 717 after deposing the usurper Theodosius III; immediately after assuming the throne he successfully resisted a yearlong Arab siege of the capital, and would repel two subsequent Arab invasions decisively, in 726 and 739. A brisk leader, he is credited with far-reaching legal reforms, including the elevation of the serfs into a free class, the abolition of certain onerous taxes, and the reform of family and maritime law.

But the policy of iconoclasm, enforced by a 730 edict against the worship of religious images and symbolized by the removal of a prominent image of Christ from the palace gates, proved disastrously unpopular throughout the empire. At home the opposition was led, at first, by Patriarch Germanus, who was subsequently deposed by Leo, although the latter took no further punitive measures against the patriarch. The policy was enforced, after Leo's death, by his son, Constantine V (reigned 741–775), and it was only after the brief rule of Constantine's son, Leo IV (reigned 775–780), and the rise to power of Leo IV's wife, Irene, who was secretly iconodule—i.e., a supporter of the veneration of icons—that the First Iconoclastic Period came to an end.

Cavafy's treatment of Leo III as a villain and his recalcitrant patriarch, Germanus, as a noble hero owes rather more to the heavily biased chronicles of the Constantinopolitan and iconodule monk and historian Theophanes (c. 760 to 817–18) than it does to Paparrigopoulos, who is more sympathetic to Leo's legislative reforms than his Byzantine predecessor is, and views Germanus's opposition less favorably.

It is from Theophanes' *Chronographia* (a chronicle of world events from 284 to 813) that the donnée of the present poem derives. In the chapter of his chronicle devoted to the year "6221" (that is, September 729–August 730), Theophanes relates the following curious exchange between the emperor and his patriarch—an exchange that Paparrigopoulos cites, in his own history, as evidence of how difficult it was to pin down the character of the emperor:

> In the same year the lawbreaking Emperor Leo raged against
> the true faith. He brought in the blessed Germanus and

began to entice him with wheedling words. The blessed chief prelate told him, "We have heard there will be a condemnation of the holy and revered icons, but not during your reign." When the emperor forced him to say during whose reign it would be, he replied, "Conon's." At which the Emperor said, "In fact, my baptismal name is Conon." The patriarch said, "My Lord, do not let this evil come to pass during your reign. For he who does so is the precursor of the Antichrist and the overthrower of the incarnate and divine dispensation." The tyrant became enraged at this; he put heavy pressure on the blessed man, just as Herod had once put on John the Baptist. But the patriarch reminded him of the covenants he had made before he became Emperor: he had given Germanus a pledge secured by God that he would in no way disturb God's church from its apostolic laws, which God had handed down. But the wretched man felt no shame at this. He observed Germanus and argued with him, and put forth statements to the effect that if he found Germanus opposing his rule, he would condemn the holder of the [patriarchal] throne as if he were a conspirator and not a confessor. (tr. Harry Turtledove, with some modifications)

Hunc Deorum Templis pg. 27

March 1926. The title and date appear on the first of the two sheets comprising this dossier; sheet two, containing the text of the draft, which was written swiftly and all at once, indicates that the final lines gave the poet some trouble. The variant readings stand side by side with no indication of which he preferred.

This tart little poem is based on an incident in the life of Julian for which Cavafy, as so often, made use of two sources, one ancient and the other modern. The latter was Allard's three-volume life of Julian (see above, pp. 69–70); the former was Ammianus Marcellinus (ca. 330–after 391), a contemporary of Julian's whose immense thirty-one-volume history covered the span from the death of the emperor Nerva in 98 to the death of Valens in 378. A pagan, Ammianus was, unsurprisingly, a great partisan of Julian's, in whose campaigns in both the east and the west he took part; Gibbon approvingly judged him "an accurate and faithful guide, who composed the history of his own times without indulging the prejudices and passions which usually affect the mind of a contemporary." Ammianus reports an incident that allegedly took place early in 356, when Julian, recently elevated to the rank of *caesar* by the emperor, his cousin Constantius, was sent north to put down incursions by German tribes along the Rhine frontier. According to Ammianus, the young Julian was rapturously received by the citizens of Vienne, who, impressed by the royal splendor of his entrance, were relieved to see that this was no usurper but a legitimate prince. As the crowds acclaimed Julian, Ammianus goes on, "a blind old woman, on enquiring who it was who was entering the town and being told that it was Caesar Julian, exclaimed that this was the man who would restore the temples of the gods [*hunc templa deorum reparaturum*]."

The exquisite ambivalence that hovers over the present poem—was the blind old woman a secret pagan cheering the secretly pagan Julian on, or a perceptive Christian denouncing him (rumors of his anti-Christian inclinations having spread from the east)?—derives from Cavafy's reading of Allard. Citing evidence from inscriptions, the French historian (1.393ff) reminds his readers that despite the presence of a vigorous Christian cell there, the pagan gods remained popular in Vienne at that time; and he recalls, too, that communication between the Greek east and the city would not have been as difficult as it might first appear (1.397): hence the possibility that locals might have heard about Julian's pagan tendencies. Given this, Allard takes the old woman in Ammianus's story—providing the story is true, which he acknowledges may well not be the case—to be one of Vienne's loyal pagans.

The motif of secret identities revealed through a kind of telepathy connects this poem to others in the Cavafian corpus, among which not only another of the Unfinished Poems about Julian ("The Bishop Pegasius," in which secret paganism is concentric, one strongly feels, with secret homosexuality), but also, for instance, the Published Poem "He Asked About the Quality," a poem, set in the poet's own time, in which the secret is clearly homosexual yearning. For Cavafy's interest in tele-

pathic knowledge more generally, see "Among the Groves of the Prom-
enades" and "Athanasius," with notes.

The title of this poem preserves Cavafy's incorrect rendering of the
blind woman's exclamation in Ammianus's tale (*templis* instead of the
text's *templa*).

The back of the page on which the text of this poem appears offers
the following variant for the final two lines:

> did you say it—as was fitting—in sorrow
> or in joy, abominable old woman?

The reading Lavagnini has adopted is less overtly editorial.

Crime

pg. 28

July 1927. The dossier for this poem contains, apart from the covering
sheet, four heavily worked sheets of text. Sheet 2 contains the text of an
early form of the poem (see below); both sides of sheet 3 contain the
text of what appears to be the last form, with very few corrections; a
fourth sheet contains very few variant line readings, noted below; and
the fifth sheet contains drafts of the final stanza.

There is some question as to whether the final stanza actually belongs
to this poem. However, its presence in the dossier, along with the fact
that the device of a "frame" chronologically later than the event
described in the body of the poem is so well attested in Cavafy's work
(see the commentary on "Ptolemy the Benefactor [or Malefactor]," and
also on "Epitaph of a Samian"), argue strongly for its being a part of this
very strong work. The date mentioned in this frame is, indeed, a matter
to which the poet gave no little thought: Lavagnini's reconstruction of
the text indicates that he first considered 1896, then a suggestively
unspecified date in the 1890s ("The one is barely visible; then eight,
then nine / The fourth numeral is faded away"), then 1916, then 1919.
As the poet clearly understood, the much later date achieves a far
stronger emotional effect, further isolating the character of the mature,
indeed even elderly poet from the scene of his dangerous youthful
milieu and passionate erotic affair.

Cavafy's fascination with the lives of beautiful youths living at the fringes of society, possibly criminal, is reflected in many poems throughout his career. Curiously, a number of these seem to have been written in the mid- to late 1910s, the moment to which the poet, in the present poem, assigns the poetic framing device. "That's How" (*1913*) expresses no little fascination—prurient, for all its aghast protestations—with the life of a street youth who's posed for a pornographic photograph:

> Who knows what debased, sordid life you must lead;
> how horrid the setting must have been
> when you posed so they could photograph you;
> what a tawdry soul yours must be.
> But given all of this, and more, to me you remain
> the face that comes in dreams, a figure
> fashioned for and dedicated to Greek pleasure—

A few years later the poet turns to a rough but touchingly passionate group of youths, strongly reminiscent of the one described in "Felony," in "In a City of Osrhoene" (*1916*; *1917*). Here the narrator similarly describes a touching solidarity among violent gang members:

> From the tavern brawl they brought him back to us, wounded—
> our friend Rhemon, around midnight yesterday.
> Through the windows we'd left open all the way
> the moon illumined his beautiful body on the bed.
> We're a hodgepodge here: Syrians, Greeks, Armenians, Medes.
> Rhemon too is such a one.

The Unpublished Poem "The Bandaged Shoulder" (*1919*) also hints that a desirable young man has been involved in illicit, and in this case violent, activities:

> He said that he'd hit a wall, or that he'd fallen.
> But probably there was another reason
> for the wounded, bandaged shoulder.

Already in a note of 1906, Cavafy had acknowledged the fascination that lower-class youths held for him, in language that is highly suggestive, given the criminal milieu that also exerted no little appeal for him:

> I do like and I am moved by the beauty of the folk, of the poor youth. Servants, workers, petty commercial clerks, shop attendants. This is the recompense, one guesses, for their deprivations. . . . They are a contrast to the affluent youth who are either sickly and physiologically dirty, or filled with fat and stains from too much food and drink, and [comfortable] quilts; you think that in their bloated or dimpled faces you can discern the ugliness of the theft and robbery of their inheritance and its interest.

The appeal that such figures had for him is evident in the last year of his poetic creation. In "Days of 1908" (*1932*; 1932), the narrator lingeringly describes the beauty of a youth whose rather grand rejection of a low-level clerk's job has forced him to find other, more marginal ways of making a living:

> Two or three shillings a day was what he'd get, sometimes not.
> What could the boy possibly earn from cards and backgammon
> in the coffee-houses of his class, the common ones,
> however cleverly he played, however stupid the partners he chose?
> And loans—there were those loans.
> It was rare that he'd manage a crown, more often it was half;
> sometimes he'd settle for shillings.

This poem is perhaps also worth thinking about in the context of a discussion of "Felony" because in it we find again the structure of an erotic reverie about low-class youth considered from the poetic vantage point of a much later date. Indeed, an earlier version of it, entitled "The Summer of 1895," was probably written around 1921, which suggests that not only that special social and erotic milieu, but more specifically that particular structure, were much on the poet's mind from the late 1910s through the 1920s.

Other significant variant readings are as follows:

LINE 2   the best lad in our gang

LINE 3A   and the one who'd been my lover for two years

LINE 8   We persuaded him. Poor thing, he
                      offered to hold a third of it for safekeeping

LINE 15   When we'd decided on a plan for his escape

LINE 16   the other two

OR   the other two [or three] (who worked as carpenters)

LINE 17   at six

LINE 23   that these were the final hours of our love

OR   that this was the final night of our love

Of the Sixth or Seventh Century   *pg. 30*

December 1927. The first of the four sheets in this dossier bears the title and the date; the third contains the last form of the poem with only two small corrections; and the second and third contain the variants to the opening, along with some other variant line readings.

In the autumn of 641, having already conquered the Byzantine strongholds of Jerusalem, Antioch, Aleppo, Damascus, and a number of other cities in a series of stunning victories, Arab forces led by Amr Ibn-el-'Aas, the great general of the caliph Omar I, advanced on Alexandria. After harassing the great port city for nearly a year, Amr finally negotiated a treaty with the Byzantine viceroy, the patriarch Cyrus; in September 642, Arab soldiers entered the city of "four thousand palaces, four thousand baths, and four hundred theaters," barely able to contain their admiration for the lavish capital. ("The moonlight reflected from the white marble made the city so bright," one is reported to have marveled, "that a tailor could see to thread his needle without a lamp. No one entered the city without having a covering on his eyes to veil him from the glare of the plaster and marble.") On the caliph's orders, the entire collection of the Library of Alexandria—except for the works of Aristotle—was burned as fuel to heat water for the public baths.

Already in a position to look back at that climactic moment in the long twilight of Hellenic culture, the narrator of this poem articulates, with an unusually naked emotionality made poignant by his consciousness of the ultimate decline of Classical civilization, his allegiance to Greek civilization—its culture and, particularly, its language. For that reason, this Poem has perhaps even more in common with works such as the Unpublished Poem "Poseidonians" (*1906*) and the Unfinished "Epitaph of a Samian," in which devotees of Greek culture hang on to whatever shreds of Greek they can retain, than it does with those poems that are specifically concerned with the sixth or seventh centuries A.D. in Alexandria: "If Indeed He Died," the early, 1897 draft of which was reworked in 1910 and 1920; "For Ammon, Who Died at 29 in 610," written and revised between 1915 and 1917; and "Aemilian son of Monaës, Alexandrian, 628–655 A.D.," an early draft of which dates back to 1898, and which found its final form in 1918. The combination of resignation and yearning also colors "Fugitives" (*1914*), in which the two exiles from Constantinople skulk around the Egyptian capital; as Lavagnini notes, what makes the present poem unique is that the city itself occupies the foreground here, as a character in and of itself.

The variants for the opening lines are as follows:

On sheet 2:

> My imagination takes me now
> to the Alexandria not of the Ptolemies,
> but of the fifth or sixth century.
>
> I love her every form and epoch

and on sheet 4:

> How moving is the Alexandria
> of its final era. Of the sixth
> century, or the beginning of the seventh
> before the Arab power came.

Sheet 4 also offers a striking variant reading of the second stanza, which indicates that Cavafy had thought at one point of making the narrator a poet:

It's not unnatural if I so feelingly
gaze at this period of hers
I who am a Greek poet, —a Greek, who on my own
have made my Greek opus on her soil

Tigranocerta   pg. 31

May 1929. The first of the three sheets that make up this dossier bears
the title and the date; the second contains the text of the poem, which
was written with apparent speed and very few corrections (all of which
belong to the first five lines); the third bears seven lines of fragmentary
variant readings.

The poem refers to events of the first century B.C., and owes its
ironic bite to an episode recounted by Plutarch in his life of the Roman
general Lucullus. TIGRANOCERTA was the southern capital of Armenia,
founded by TIGRANES I "THE GREAT," the so-called King of Kings of a
short-lived Armenian empire. Established on the Armenian throne in
100 B.C., Tigranes soon demonstrated a passion for power, pomp, and
expansionism. Allying himself with Mithridates, the king of Pontus, he
ravaged the territories of Media in central Asia and seized northern
Mesopotamia from the Parthians; in 83 B.C. he took over Syria, Phoeni-
cia, and Cilicia. Those Greek cities that sided with him were treated
indulgently, but those that resisted were reduced and their inhabitants
transferred to the opulent new capital of Tigranocerta. Plutarch, who
as we know was a favorite of Cavafy's (his friend I. A. Sarayannis, in his
1964 *Notes on Cavafy,* recalled how the poet would often sprinkle his
conversation with citations from the biographer) is clearly the source
for this poem, and goes out of his way to emphasize the hubristic arro-
gance of the self-made King of Kings:

> Above all, the spirit of the king himself had become pompous
> and haughty in the midst of his great prosperity. Not only did
> he possess all that men covet and admire most, but he actually
> thought that they existed for his sake. For although he had
> begun his career with small and insignificant expectations, he
> had conquered many nations. . . . Many were the kings who
> waited upon him; four, whom he always kept about him like

attendants or bodyguards, would run on foot, wearing short tunics, by their master's side when he rode out, and when he sat transacting business, they would stand by with their arms crossed.

In view of the present poem's somewhat skeptical view of Hellenic culture as it survived throughout the world long after Alexander's conquests—a theme found in "Philhellene" (1906; 1912) and many other poems—it is noteworthy that Plutarch attributed to the inhabitants of Tigranocerta the same overweening arrogance shown by its king: "It was a rich and beautiful city," he writes, "every common man, and every man of rank, in imitation of the king, studied to enlarge and adorn it." One senses, from "Tigranocerta," that this enthusiasm among the people of Tigranocerta to adorn the capital with Greek culture has not made them the more discriminating.

Tigranes' grandiosity, particularly as reflected in his aggressive expansionism, was always an irritant to Rome, and eventually led to all-out war. In 69 B.C. Lucullus utterly crushed the Armenians and reduced Tigranocerta, an overwhelming victory all the more noteworthy for its contrast with the pretensions of the Armenian leader: Plutarch put the Armenian dead at over a hundred thousand, with only a hundred Romans wounded and five killed, and cited other sources, among them Strabo and Livy, on the remarkable nature of the victory ("The Romans never fought an enemy with such unequal resources, for the conquerors were not so much as one-twentieth part of the number of the conquered").

The ironic contrast between the king's pretension and the cruel reality that awaits him will, in fact, be mirrored by the experience of Cavafy's cocky speaker—although he cannot yet know it. Renata Lavagnini identifies a passing reference in chapter 29 of Plutarch's account as the source of Cavafy's inspiration; it is easy to see how this short passage provided not only the idea for the narrator, but also the larger framework (with its hint at this amateur actor's possible fate) within which the poem must be understood:

In the city Tigranocerta, meanwhile, the Greeks, having separated themselves from the barbarians, attempted to hand the city over to Lucullus, who attacked and took it. He himself seized the treasure; the city he gave to his soldiers to be sacked, and in it were found eight thousand talents in coin money, along with other possessions. In addition to this, he distributed eight hundred drachmas to each man out of the spoils. When he learned that among the prisoners of the city were many actors whom Tigranes had invited from all over for the opening of the theatre he had built, Lucullus used them to celebrate his triumphal games and spectacles.

Our awareness of the looming disaster—with which the speaker, so typically in Cavafy, is blithely unconcerned, preoccupied as he is with his grandiose personal fantasies—clearly connects this poem to others in the corpus. George Savidis pointed out that it bears a certain resemblance to "Young Men of Sidon," which like this poem is set just before the demise of the world so intensely celebrated by its characters. Similarly, in "In 200 B.C.," the Greek speaker's vainglorious championing of Greek achievements is framed, ironically, by our knowledge that within a few years Rome would decisively crush Greek forces both in Greece and in Asia, thereby establishing its supremacy once and for all. See also the note on "Epitaph of a Samian," p. 87–90.

Variants:

LINE 3	cousin
LINE 14	one or two rich men
LINE 23	I'll stay here for five months

Abandonment pg. 32

May 1930. The dossier consists of three sheets, the first of which bears the title and the date. Sheet 2 contains drafts of the first two stanzas, with variants and corrections, and sheet 3 contains the text of the entire poem, with some corrections as well; the back of sheet 3 contains verses that Lavagnini believes were deleted from the Published Poem "Come, O King of the Lacedaemonians" (1929).

Two deletions are worthy of attention. To the word "abandonment" in line 4 the poet had originally added the phrase "complete and utter"; and an earlier version of the second line of the second stanza read, "Perhaps it shouldn't last any longer."

The poem presents a character—the cocky young man whose superciliousness is a cover for tenderer feelings that he cannot seem to admit to consciousness—familiar from other works, such as the Published Poem "In the Taverns" (1926). See too the note on "Above All Cynegirus," pp. 41–5.

Nothing About the Lacedaemonians   *pg. 33*

July 1930. The entire poem is written on one sheet; a covering sheet bears the title. The latter indicates that Cavafy had considered an alternate version of the title, "Except for the Lacedaemonians"; the phrase reveals the deep and complex significance of the title, and of the poem as a whole—and indeed this poem's relationship to other works in the Cavafian corpus.

The opening line is a quotation from the message from Alexander the Great to the Athenians that accompanied the three hundred Persian panoplies that he sent to Athens to commemorate his victory over the forces of Darius III, the king of Persia—a line that, according to the protocols of Ancient Greek inscriptions, constituted what we might today refer to as the "from" line:

ALEXANDER, SON OF PHILIP,
AND THE GREEKS EXCEPT FOR THE LACEDAEMONIANS . . .

"Except for the Lacedaemonians" pointedly alludes to the fact that of the Greek states, only Sparta (also known as Lacedaemon) refused to join in Alexander's panhellenic campaign against Persia, proudly unwilling, as they were, to serve under a non-Spartan general. And yet this ostensibly high-minded and nationalistic pride cost the militaristic Lacedaemonians dearly, since in refusing to join the Macedonian's expedition into Asia, they missed out on the greatest military conquests the world had ever seen: conquests that took Alexander and his armies as far east as Bactria, a province located in what is now the northern part of present-day Afghanistan, and India.

Alexander's rebuke to the Spartans had been on Cavafy's mind for fifteen years by the time he wrote the present poem. The original title of "In 200 B.C.," first composed in 1916 and published in 1931, was, in fact, "Except the Lacedaemonians." In that earlier poem, the narrator cites Alexander's text and goes on to sneer at the Spartans' proud isolationism; with unmistakable pride, he lists the many victories that Alexander and his forces managed to achieve "without the Lacedaemonians"—a tart rebuke to the Spartan position. But as the Cavafy scholar and translator Edmund Keeley pointed out long ago in his 1976 study *Cavafy's Alexandria,* the date of 200 B.C. suggests an ironic undercutting of the speaker's Hellenic swagger: within ten years of that date, the Greek Hellenistic monarchies of Macedon and Asia—the heirs of Alexander—would crumble under the onslaught of Roman forces, and all that had been Greater Greece would become the property of Rome.

The invocation of Alexander's words clearly serves a similar purpose in the present poem (where they are paraphrased as "nothing about the Lacedaemonians," an alteration that gives the phrase the quality of an axiom), illuminating a theme to which the poet returns so often: the way in which the eventualities of history can ironize men's intellectual, cultural, and political pretensions. The speaker here, like that in the earlier poem, looks back condescendingly on the Spartans' refusal to fight under a foreign general, which he sees as overprincipled. And yet, as we know from other poems in the corpus that belong to the same period of composition as this one—for instance, "In Sparta" (1928) and "Come Now, King of the Lacedaemonians" (1929)—Cavafy himself had tremendous admiration for the unyieldingly high principles shown by the Spartans, particularly, as those two poems make clear, when adhered to in times of abject defeat. Understood within the densely allusive network to which the use of Alexander's phrase, and the allusion to Spartan principles, should alert us, the present poem therefore suggests that it is the speaker, rather than the Lacedaemonians to whom he condescends here, who should be considered a fool.

A variant for line 8 reads, "What a lover of the truth, an equable man!"

Zenobia

November 1930. Apart from the covering sheet, which bears the title and date, there is only one sheet, which shows signs of great vacillation on the poet's part; the end of the last line is illegible, as indicated by the crosses (each of which stands for approximately two letters).

ZENOBIA (ca. 240–after 274) was the alluring and canny queen of the short-lived Palmyrene empire: caught between empires and cultures, combining great charm and immense ambition, and claiming an illustrious Alexandrian lineage to boot, she was a type of post-Classical character so greatly appreciated by Cavafy. Much of her history is related by the Byzantine historian Zosimus in his *New History*.

During the period of internal weakness and external collapse known as the Crisis of the Third Century, the Roman Empire split into three enormous sections: the easternmost of these arced along the Mediterranean coast from the southern part of present-day Turkey to the northern part of Egypt. After the Syrian king who had consolidated most of these territories under his rule, Odaenathus, was assassinated in 266–67, his beautiful and ambitious widow, Zenobia, took control of the empire in the name of their infant son. During her brief rule, more territories were added, and Zenobia went so far as to assume the title *Augusta,* "Empress."

By 270 Rome's crisis was nearing its end under the leadership of the emperor Aurelian; after dispensing with the rebellious provinces in the west of Europe, he turned his attention to the east, and in 272 he defeated Zenobia's armies at the Battles of Immae (near Antioch) and Emesa. A story that emerged from these crushing defeats reveals much about Zenobia's character: it is said that after losing to the Romans at Immae, she fled to Antioch ahead of the news, presenting herself to the city as the victor, accompanied by a man resembling Aurelian who was weighted down by chains—a maneuver that bought her enough time to flee in the night. After Emesa she tried to flee again, this time to her former enemies the Persians, but was captured. Interestingly—perhaps because he was impressed by her—Aurelian granted clemency to Zenobia (who appeared in golden chains at his triumph in Rome), and she ended her days in comfortable exile at Rome, where she took up philosophy and acted the Roman matron.

Although born into prominent enough circumstances—her father was a Syrian chieftain who could boast of genealogical ties to the Roman empress Julia Domna—Zenobia appears to have had no qualms about enhancing the allure of her family tree. Among other things, she claimed descent from Drusilla of Mauretania, the great-granddaughter of the Egyptian queen Cleopatra, who belonged to the LAGID dynasty and who was, through her descent from Alexander's general Ptolemy, of MACEDONIAN descent. (For instance, the *Historia Augusta* reports that, in an imperial declaration of the year 269 addressed to the people of Alexandria, Zenobia referred to the city as "my ancestral city.")

Although the French scholar of Hellenistic history Bouché-Leclercq (well known to Cavafy) and Gibbon both make reference to Zenobia's genealogical pretensions, which suggest the kind of personality much beloved of Cavafy, the poet-historian devoted to post-Classical history, the figure of the Syrian queen was likely to have interested him for other reasons. One tale told concerning Aurelian's reconquest of the eastern provinces prominently features Apollonius of Tyana, the figure so fascinating to the poet; according to this legend, Aurelian spared the city of Tyana after a vision of Apollonius appeared to him begging the emperor not to destroy it.

The state of the second part of the text for this poem is questionable at best. On the back of the sheet on which the text of this poem appears there are lines suggesting that Cavafy had toyed with the idea of elaborating the characters of the scholars charged with the task of genealogical enhancement:

> Two scholars skilled in history
> ~~Are taking up the important task~~
> See how they deal with her genealogy

Company of Four   *pg. 35*

Although the dossier for this poem, which consists of six sheets, itself bears no date, the evidence cited by Lavagnini for a date of 1930 is more than persuasive: two of the sheets bear that date; the name *Zabinas* (along with a variant, *Zebinas*) doodled on the back of sheet 2, belong to the poem "Should Have Taken the Trouble," which was first printed in

July 1930; and sheet 6 is of the same paper used by the poet early in 1930 to compose a list of titles. A parenthetical note to the covering sheet indicates that the title was to be considered "provisional."

This is the only one of the Unfinished Poems to be written in the style, recurring frequently in the Published and Unpublished Poems, which Savidis has characterized as tango-like: poems each of whose lines consists of two short rhythmical elements, each with the following meter: ∪–∪–∪–x. Cavafy uses this form almost exclusively in writing of frustrated or lost love; most of these poems were published in the mid-1920s. See, for example, "Maker of Wine Bowls" (*1903*; *1912*; *1921*), "In Despair" (*1923*; 1923), "Theater of Sidon" (*1923*; 1923), "Before Time Could Change Them" (*1924*; 1924), and "Temethus, an Antiochene: 400 A.D." (*?*; 1925).

Agelaus   pg. 36

The dossier for this poem contains seven sheets: sheet 1 gives the title and the date "Apr[il] 1932"; 2 and 3 contain the text of the poem, which bears few corrections; and the rest contain Cavafy's transcription of one of his sources for the incident narrated in the poem, on which see below.

This poem returns to a favorite Cavafian theme—the foolish short-sightedness of men who are too often hamstrung by their own narrow vision of the world (compare, for instance, "Nero's Deadline")—set at a favorite Cavafian moment: the confrontation, ultimately fatal to Greece, between the declining Greek city-states and the rising power of Rome to the west.

The Second Punic War (218–202 B.C.) between the expanding Roman Republic and its great rival in North Africa, Carthage, created a rare opportunity for the perennially warring Greek city-states to band together and, united, to confront their common enemy to the west. In the summer of 217, PHILIP V (238–179 B.C.), the dynamic if erratic ruler of Macedon and the most powerful man on the Greek mainland, was involved in a war against other Greeks—in this case, the Aetolian League. After learning of the Carthaginians' devastating defeat of the Romans at Lake Trasimene in the north of Italy, in June 217, Philip was convinced that negotiations with his fellow Greeks would be advanta-

geous, and a peace conference thereafter took place at the port city of
NAUPACTUS, on the Gulf of Corinth. Here, according to the historian
Polybius, one of the Aetolian delegates, AGELAUS, gave a rousing speech
in which he showed a prescient understanding for the necessity of a
concerted Greek front against Rome. His advice was heeded, but within
a few years Hellenic unity had, all too typically, become fragmented,
and in 211 Rome concluded an alliance with the Aetolians against
Philip, who was eventually crushed by the Romans under Titus Flamin-
inus at the Battle of CYNOSCEPHALAE in 197. Cynoscephalae would
turn out to be the first of three decisive defeats by Rome of Greek
states: in 190, L. Cornelius Scipio and his brother, Scipio Africanus,
trounced the forces of the Seleucid king Antiochus III at the Battle of
MAGNESIA, and in 168 the Roman general L. Aemilius Paullus crushed
Philip V's son, Perseus, at the Macedonian city of PYDNA, thereby
putting an end forever to the Macedonian dynasty descended from
Alexander's general, Antigonus the One-Eyed. Together, the defeats at
Cynoscephalae, Magnesia, and Pydna mark the end of Greek power in
the Mediterranean and Near East.

Cavafy had two sources for Agelaus's words at the conference of
Naupactus, one ancient and the other modern. The former was the
account of Polybius (5.103), whose version of Agelaus's speech Cavafy
closely follows:

> The Greeks should not go to war with each other at all. . . .
> For even now it is evident to any one who pays even moder-
> ate attention to public affairs, that whether the Carthaginians
> conquer the Romans, or the Romans the Carthaginians, it is
> in every way improbable that the victors will remain con-
> tented with the empire of Sicily and Italy. They will move
> forward. . . . Wherefore, I beseech you all to be on your
> guard against the danger of the crisis, and above all you, O
> King . . . consult on the contrary for their good as you
> would for your own person, and have a care for all parts of
> Greece alike, as part and parcel of your own domains. . . . If
> you are eager for action, turn your eyes to the west, and let
> your thoughts dwell upon the wars in Italy.

Cavafy's contemporary source was an article by the British historian W. W. Tarn in *The Cambridge Ancient History, 7: The Hellenistic Monarchies and the Rise of Rome,* a long extract of which Cavafy transcribed by hand and kept in the dossier for the present poem. The reference to Cynoscephalae, Magnesia, and Pydna in the second stanza makes it clear that, however rousing the "delusive gleam" (as Tarn put it) of the Aeolian's exhortation to the assembled Greeks, the proper context for understanding the poem is our awareness of the disastrous events that followed, which indeed fulfilled the dark prophecy uttered by Agelaus at the end of his speech, a passage not paraphrased in Cavafy's poem but copied into his notes for it:

> If the cloud rising in the west once overspreads Greece, we shall, I fear, no longer play the games which now like children we play together, rather shall we be praying to the gods to give us back the chance of fighting and make peace with each other when we choose, and even of calling our very quarrels our own.

For this reason, the end of the third century B.C.—and in particular the date 200 B.C.—has an especially dark and ironic resonance in Cavafy's work, coming as it does just before the end of Greek political significance in the ancient world: see, for instance, "In 200 B.C." and "In a Great Greek Colony, 200 B.C." Other poems that refer to the decline of Greek fortunes in the first half of the second century B.C. include "The Battle of Magnesia," "For Antiochus Epiphanes," "The Seleucid's Displeasure," and "Envoys from Alexandria."

APPENDIX

The Fragmentary Sketches

The Cavafy Archive contains a number of sketches that the poet did not collect into dossiers; Professor Lavagnini has identified these as being the fragmentary material of four discrete poems. They have no titles, and there is no sign that Cavafy considered them to be works in progress on a par, either practically or aesthetically, with the Unfinished drafts. Indeed, this fragmentary material suggests, by implication, something important about the thirty Unfinished drafts: that Cavafy only assembled dossiers when he felt that a poem had "taken"—that it was, indeed, fully on its way to being a poem. For this reason, I am offering translations here of the reconstructed sketches with a bare minimum of commentary—the latter to remind readers, as it were, that we should not get too close to work that is in every way partial. As this poet knew so well, one effect of Time is that some things get lost in it, and as a result remain truly and irrecoverably "unfinished." That we must recognize this is one of the harder lessons that History, and Cavafy's poetry, teach us.

[Bondsman and Slave]

A bondsman and a slave, a stranger to pleasure,
bent at the same task for forty years
over his bench, he lines up the new
coins that the people of Nicaea issue.
He'll hold up one, another he'll measure;
and attentively, his eyes fogged by old age,
he examines them to make sure the inscription is true.
If he makes another mistake, they said, he'll be tortured,
and his hands are trembling.
"With Severus as king the world enjoys good fortune."*

*The last line is the actual legend on a coin minted during the reign of Septimius Severus (145–211 A.D.), the first emperor to be born in Africa and the founder of the short-lived and troubled Severan dynasty; his wife was Julia Domna, the patroness of Philostratus, author of *The Life of Apollonius of Tyana* and of *The Lives of the Sophists,* two favorite texts of Cavafy's.

[Colors]

The scarlets, the yellows, and the blues
of flowers are beautiful, I'll admit.
But whenever I imagine what color is,
color that is fixed and unpolluted,
it's not to flowers that my mind turns, but
to the scarlet of rubies and of coral,
to the yellow of topaz and of gold,
and of sapphires and turquoise the blue.

[My Soul Was on My Lips]

There was absolutely nothing romantic
in the way he said "Perhaps I'll die."
He said it as a joke. Just the way a boy
of three and twenty years will say such things.
And I—at twenty-five—took it casually.
Nothing (fortunately) of the mock-sentimental poetry
that moves the fashionable ladies (laughable)
who blubber over nothing.

And nevertheless when I found myself outside the
doorway of the house
I had the notion that it wasn't a joke.
He could indeed be dying. And with that fear in mind
I climbed the steps at a run; it was the third floor.
And without our exchanging a single word,
I kissed his forehead, his eyes, his mouth,
his chest, his hands, and every single limb;
so that I imagined—as Plato's heavenly lines
have it—that my soul came to my lips.

I didn't go to the funeral. I was sick.
All alone his mother mourned for him,
over the white coffin, pure of heart.*

*The lines in question are from an epigram in the *Palatine Anthology* (a vast collection of
Greek poetry, epigrams, drinking songs, and erotic verse from the Classical through the
Byzantine period). Attributed to Plato, it makes a reference to the famously effeminate
dramatic playwright Agathon, whose victory party (he had won the tragic competition)
is the setting for Plato's *Symposium:* "When I kissed Agathon, I had my soul upon my lips
/ for it came, poor wretch, and made as if to pass over."

[Matthew First, First Luke]

Fifteen years had already passed.
It was the first year of Theodosius's reign.
In the salon of his father's mansion
a young man, an Alexandrian, was waiting
for a visit from his beloved friend.

In order to pass the time more easily
he started to read the first book he came across.

It was by a very tetchy sophist
who, as a slight to the Christians,
quoted the sentence of Julian.
"Certainly" the young Alexandrian murmured,
"Matthew first, first Luke."

Still, as for the rest of Julian's trivialities,
Homer and Hesiod, he merely smiled.*

*A widely reviled edict promulgated by the emperor Julian in the summer of 362 forbade the teaching of the pagan classics by Christians. The passage to which these lines refer contains Julian's notoriously contemptuous dismissal of Christian scholars: "Was it not the gods who revealed all their learning to Homer, Hesiod, Demosthenes? . . . If they [the Christian teachers] think that those writers were in error concerning the honored gods, then let them go to the Galileans' churches to expound upon Matthew and Luke. . . ." The edict was revoked by Theodosius I. The tetchy sophist is probably Libanius, a friend and ardent supporter of Julian's, who was nonetheless honored by Theodosius.

FURTHER READING

The following books will be of value to the general reader interested in further exploring Cavafy's life, work, and intellectual world:

The Mind and Art of C. P. Cavafy (Denise Harvey & Co., 1983). An appealingly diverse collection of the classic essays on Cavafy and his work by E. M. Forster, George Seferis, Patrick Leigh Fermor, W. H. Auden, and others.

G. W. Bowersock. *Julian the Apostate* (Harvard University Press, 1978). A refreshingly brisk and vigorous short study of the historical figure who fascinated Cavafy more than any other.

Peter Brown. *The World of Late Antiquity AD 150–750* (W. W. Norton, 1989). An expansive survey of the history and culture of a period that represents one of Cavafy's historial "margins"—long neglected by traditional classicists but of paramount interest to the poet.

E. M. Forster. *Alexandria: A History and a Guide* (1922; repr. Oxford, 1986). A survey *cum* guidebook that savors seductively of Cavafy's own era, by the English novelist who befriended Cavafy there during World War I, and who was responsible for first bringing the poet to the attention of English readers and critics. (With an Introduction by Lawrence Durrell, whose *Alexandria Quartet* is required reading for anyone interested in the city that shaped Cavafy's poetry.)

Peter Green. *The Hellenistic Age* (Modern Library Chronicles, 2007). An excellent brief introduction to the era that provided a setting for so many of Cavafy's poems; for those not daunted by its thousand pages, the same author's magisterial *Alexander to Actium: The Historical Evolution of the Hellenistic Age* (California, 1993) provides a magnificently detailed yet admirably lively account of the period.

Edmund Keeley. *Cavafy's Alexandria* (1976; repr. Princeton University Press, 1995). A meticulous analysis of the Cavafian corpus by the eminent translator and scholar, with a special emphasis on the crucial symbolic role of the city in the poet's work.

R. Liddell. *Cavafy: A Biography* (Duckworth, 1974; repr. 2000). Workmanlike but packed with useful information, this is still the only book-length biography of the poet in English.

John Julius Norwich. *A Short History of Byzantium* (Knopf, 1998). The abridged version of Norwich's magisterial three-volume study is the best popular introduction to the history of the Empire.

Philostratus, edited and translated by C. P. Jones. *Apollonius of Tyana* (Loeb Classical Library, 2006). This new translation brings to vivid life the sprawling quasi-novel that Cavafy considered a "storehouse of poetic material."

ACKNOWLEDGMENTS

For the opportunity to bring the Unfinished Poems to English speakers, I am enormously grateful and immeasurably indebted to Manuel Savidis; grateful, too, for his warm support and long-distance friendship over several years now; and for permission to quote from his translations of Cavafy's "Notes on Poetics and Ethics" as well as other material in the Archive.

A number of individuals offered crucial advice and support as I worked on preparing this volume; a special debt of gratitude is owed to Pavlos Sfyroeras and Maria Hatjigeorgiou; to Robin Desser and to Lydia Wills; to Christopher Jones for permission to quote from his translation of Philostratus, and for innumerable improving suggestions; and above all to the incomparable Glen Bowersock, *sine quo non*.

Much of my work on the Unfinished Poems was made possible by a grant from the John Simon Guggenheim Memorial Foundation, which I gratefully acknowledge herewith.

INDEX OF TITLES

Daniel Mendelsohn was born on Long Island in 1960 and studied Classics at the University of Virginia and at Princeton, where he received his doctorate in 1994. His reviews and essays on literary and cultural subjects appear regularly in numerous publications, including *The New Yorker,* the *New York Times,* and *The New York Review of Books.* His previous books include *The Elusive Embrace,* a *New York Times* Notable Book and a *Los Angeles Times* Best Book of the Year, and the international best seller *The Lost: A Search for Six of Six Million,* which won the National Book Critics Circle Award, the Prix Médicis, and many other honors. Mr. Mendelsohn is also the recipient of a Guggenheim Fellowship, the National Book Critics Circle Citation for Excellence in Book Reviewing, and the George Jean Nathan Award for Dramatic Criticism. He teaches at Bard College.

A NOTE ON THE TYPE

The text of this book was set in a typeface named Perpetua, designed by the British artist Eric Gill (1882–1940) and cut by the Monotype Corporation of London in 1928–30. The shapes of the roman letters basically derive from stonecutting, a form of lettering in which Gill was eminent. The italic is essentially an inclined roman. The general effect of the typeface in reading sizes is one of lightness and grace. The larger display sizes of the type are extremely elegant and form what is one of the most distinguished series of inscriptional letters cut in the twentieth century.

Composed by North Market Street Graphics,
Lancaster, Pennsylvania
Printed and bound by R. R. Donnelley,
Crawfordsville, Indiana
Designed by Wesley Gott